Maine
&Me

Maine & Me

Ten Years of Down East Adventures

by Elizabeth Peavey

Down East Books
Camden / Maine

Copyright © 2004 by Elizabeth Peavey
All rights reserved.

ISBN 0-89272-669-5

Cover photograph by William Hubbell
Cover design by Rich Eastman

Printed at Versa Press, East Peoria, IL

5   4   3   2

Down East Books
Camden, ME
A division of Down East Enterprise, Inc.,
publishers of *Down East* magazine
Book orders: 800-766-1670
www.downeastbooks.com

Library of Congress Control Number: 2004109059

*This book is dedicated to my parents,
Shirley and the late H. William Peavey—
true Mainers, through and through*

Acknowledgements

When you have spent your entire life writing and you publish your first book at the age of forty-five, the people you need to thank could, well, fill a book. Let it suffice to say none of my writing life would've been possible without the love and support of my friends and family—especially my mom for reading every word I've ever written and my big brothers, Jim and Jeff, for keeping an eye on their kid sister. Of course, I am indebted to the folks at Down East Books for taking on this project, the editors at *Down East* magazine for sending me on all these adventures, and all the great people of the state I've met along the way. And, finally, my best thanks go to my husband: The only thing better than exploring Maine together is coming home to you. ILYML.

Foreword

Anyone who grows up in Maine and has a lick of sense generally has one supreme goal: To get out. If you're from Maine and, by chance or by choice, you end up as an adult living in Maine, you run the risk of being labeled a loser.

Sure, Maine's a great place to call home, providing you're from somewhere else. There's a certain unspoken cachet—a sense of pioneering derring-do—in moving to Maine, and transplants love this state with steadfast devotion. They're first in line in January for reservations at Baxter State Park. They never miss the Common Ground Fair. Their Subaru Outbacks sport loon conservation plates and Maine Public Radio window decals. They get all moony at the mere mention of fresh seafood (which makes me want to poke them in the eye with a Mrs. Paul's fishstick). They pick and preserve berries in season, snowshoe or cross-country ski in winter, and kayak in summer. They buy their produce at farmers' markets and know Gulf Hagas was not named for a Scottish offal dish that is boiled in a sheep's stomach.

They are, in a word, nouveau Mainers.

Now, don't get me wrong. I'm no xenophobe. Most of my closest friends are, in fact, "from away." I even married a non-native. (Okay, so he moved to Maine when he was eight years old, but still . . .)

It's just that I feel I get a bit of attitude from these transplants. Because I don't look like I'm from Maine (with the exception of my woodswear, it's all black clothing all the time) or sound like I'm from Maine (I grew up in front of the TV; my accent is Walter Cronkite with a splash of Captain Kangaroo), I'm frequently asked where I'm from. When they find out I'm a native, they give me that up-and-down look that tells me they view me as lacking. That my choice to live here was through a character defect. That I wasn't quite capable of making it anywhere else. That I was weaned on potatoes and Allen's coffee brandy—which is, of course, ridiculous. Everyone knows one doesn't serve a cordial with a starch.

I hate to admit it—especially as someone who has made a career out of flying in the face of, well, everything—but this scrutiny can roil up old insecurities in me. I know I owe no one an explanation for my decision to live in Maine, but these assessments put me on the defensive. And that is because, for most of my youth, I couldn't have agreed more.

This feeling was especially poignant growing up in the small mid-coast town of Bath, home of the Bath Iron Works. As pretty a little city as it is today, during my formative years it was a mill town. Everyone seemed to be related, even if it was in a second-cousin, twice-removed fashion. Most of my teachers were Mainers, many locals. The majority of my classmates' dads worked at the Yard (as BIW is called). When the company had its annual family day at Small Point Beach, tumbleweeds all but tossed down Front Street. While my parents were from Maine, they were not from Bath. I had no local relatives. My father was not employed by BIW. I did not attend the picnics. Because I could not join their reindeer games, I made it my goal to be nothing like my townsfolk.

In the hands of another Maine writer, this story would have a gorier resolution involving a spoiled prom night. My answer, however, was flight. My wanderlust began the moment I could point my scooter down the hill on which we lived. I remember once being referred to as "that girl from up the street" by one of the neighborhood moms. It sounded glamorous, dangerous even. From that moment on, I knew the traveling life was for me. After all, Out There was waiting.

My mission to unMaine myself took me around the world—from

the tip of Tasmania to the top of the Isle of Skye. It started with a Sierra Club hiking trip in the Wyoming Rockies in high school. When the time for choosing a college came around, I blindly and hastily selected the University of Denver, applied, and was accepted. All that remained was the agonizing wait.

You know, life is funny. You think you have it in a stranglehold, and then pow! a sucker punch, right in the kisser. For reasons that are no longer important, the Denver thing didn't happen. Instead, I was rail-roaded into attending the University of Maine at Orono. U.M. Zero. Death. I wept the entire way up that familiar route so well worn by both my older brothers before me, not for leaving home, as some do, but for not leaving home thoroughly enough.

Everyone I knew at Orono who was from Maine seemed to have an excuse for being there—a financial-aid package that didn't come through, a late application. We all complained about our fate, but few did anything about it. After three semesters, with my unMaineing clearly on the downslide, I escaped—to Portland. A baby step, but it was movement.

That was January 1979. In another year, my traveling life really began, starting with a semester in London (where I was simply referred to as "the American") and a month-long solo trek around the British Isles. The following spring, I did Europe. On trains in Italy and buses in Greece, I would sketch blobby maps of the States that looked like drunken cows and show fellow travelers where I was from. "*Maine,*" I would shout, circling the cow's head. (Shouting always helps overcome language barriers.) "*J'habite à Maine.*" (So does speaking French, even if no one else does.)

A year or so later, I loaded up my Subaru and spent four months driving solo (much to my parents' horror) around the U.S. and Canada. When I returned to Portland, it was as a citizen of the world. Maine was just a way station. I finished my degree, kicked around and then ap-plied to and got rejected by graduate school. After the sudden and un-expected death of my beloved dad and two years of grieving, flight, once again, seemed the only balm. I moved to San Francisco, where being from Maine turned out to be a boon. I was regarded as exotic, and I got tons of job interviews. Actually, they were more like *views*. "Look everyone," the H.R. representative would say, parading me in front of her colleagues, as though a moose had just wandered in off Market Street. "Miss Peavey is from *Maine*." When she said the word, she almost shouted.

Virtually everyone I knew in San Francisco was a transplant, so even though I had a California driver's license and bank account, I was still ostensibly from Maine. And then, on a trip to Australia, someone asked me where I was from and, without thinking, I responded: "San Francisco." Finally, the moment I had been waiting for all my life: To not be from Maine. But my answer sounded hollow, as though someone I didn't know had spoken for me.

Two years in San Francisco were followed by a year in Boston, but that stint was a rough one. It was 1990, and the economy and the job market had hit the skids. Playing the Maine card no longer worked. No one there found me fascinating. Or employable. Things bottomed out. After weighing my options, I looked to Maine.

I knew re-entry would be rough, especially considering each time I had left the state it was in a spray of gravel and a chorus of "So long, suckers." What, after all, could a broke, thirty-one-year-old, failed play-wright/poet with a résumé that bordered on science fiction do in a place where people who actually possessed real job skills couldn't find work? What argument could one possibly present on the side of going back? And what kind of loser, after all, gives up on the great Out There at the first sign of trouble and retreats?

Well, the answer was, this kind of loser. I wanted to go home.

Introduction

So, home I came. I'm not saying my return was all country fairs and clambakes. In fact, it was harder than I could've imagined. For the first few months, I camped out in my old room at my mother's house in Bath, skulking around the streets, terrified I would run into someone from my childhood and be asked the most dreaded question of the down-and-out: "Soooo, what are you up to these days?" I couch-surfed in my Portland friends' guest rooms (I had a key ring that looked like it belonged to a janitor) while I tried to reinvent myself. I took the scant want ads out to Fort Williams Park in the morning and pondered. I walked Back Cove in the afternoon and pondered more, ever pondering. How did this happen? Where was my lion's heart? What now? I knew how to do only two things: wait tables and write. Despite the years I had spent in the restaurant business supporting my writing habit, I was ill-suited for it and wanted out. That left writing. It had never occurred to me someone might pay me to do the thing I loved most.

Over the next couple of years, I took whatever writing-related work came my way—copyediting textbooks, jobbing up articles for an elders' newsletter, writing brochure copy, doing *pro bono* assignments for non-profits. But, at the same time, I also started exploring the state with the zeal and vigor of a transplant, seeing it as I never had before. During all those years in Portland, I barely strayed off the peninsula. When I had, it was for points south. Now, I was rediscovering all those places from my childhood—Rangeley, Moosehead, Belfast, Bar Harbor—and beyond. And as I did, I realized what I really wanted to do was write about Maine. I looked to *Down East* magazine.

I had no idea how to approach an editor or sell an idea, but I had one that I thought might fit: trying to trace whether or not I was related to Joe Peavey, the inventor of the logging tool that bears our name. I scoured all the "how-to-write-a-query" articles and books I could, put a blustery proposal together, and sent it off. Miraculously, I was given a go-ahead, and the resulting article, "Heiress Apparent"—the first in this collection—appeared in the November 1993 issue. A career was launched.

Ironically, at the same time, I was hired by the now-defunct Portland alternative paper *Casco Bay Weekly* as arts editor, and my fledgling freelance life was temporarily put on hold. I worked with excellent and talented people, learned more about writing and editing than twenty journalism degrees could've taught me, and made friends for life. Eighteen months later, however, I discovered having a "real" job—one in which you had to show up each day—wasn't for me. I left the paper, resumed freelancing, and hooked up again with *Down East* magazine.

One of my earliest assignments sent me to the North Woods and to Pittston Farm to sample the lumberjacks' buffet there. Understand, I had just started my adventuring and wasn't exactly what you would call woods savvy. Nor was my Honda Civic the ideal Golden Road vehicle—especially in early March. Plus, this was before everyone owned a cell phone (although I remain a holdout). I'm not saying that there was imminent danger involved, but a bit of cautious reserve might've been appropriate. Not for me, though. I couldn't get on the road fast enough and couldn't have been happier when I made the turn at Rockwood. I felt like I was the luckiest girl in the state of Maine.

Thousands of *Down East* miles hence, and I still feel that way. I've not once tired of looking at my state or meeting its residents and listening to their stories. Every time the phone rings and I hear my editor's voice on the other end of the line say, "Your name came up at our editorial meeting today," I get a bit of pre-lottery-drawing thrill. And if I hear myself saying, "You want me to do *what?*" or "You want me to go *where?*", I know I've hit the jackpot.

I'm proud of the courage it took to return and re-Maine myself. Home has given me my writing life. Proximity to my family. My friends. The mighty Atlantic and memories of my dad. It delivered up to this solo traveler a husband, who is also a repatriated Mainer who chose to come home. He was my companion on many of these *Down East* assignments. We courted on Maine's back roads, and he, with his characteristic good humor, grew accustomed to being referred to as "Mr. Peavey."

Over these past ten years, I've covered a lot of territory and learned a lot about how much people care for this state. And that is because I feel that whether you are from here or not, Maine ruins you for every other place. Of course, there are more glamorous locales in which to live, ones that are more electric and exotic, that have more action and culture—and, yes, more jobs. I'm glad I've seen many of them and even lived in a couple. I hope to visit more. But visiting will do. This is where I belong.

I can't tell you how much I love the state of Maine. But maybe with these stories, I can show you.

It's good to be home.

A note: I hope you will use this as a guidebook of sorts, but remember— even the most established Maine institutions (such as Pilots Grill) are subject to the winds of change. Please check to make sure any destination of interest is still operating before venturing out. Trust me, it's a long way to Matinicus and Fort Kent.

Contents

Part One: You Want Me to Do *What?*

Part Two: You Want Me to Go *Where*?

Part One

You Want Me to Do *What?*

Heiress Apparent

It's Christmas Eve. Aunt Dot is trying once again to interest my teenage nephew in the story of the invention of the peavey, the log-driving tool that, she claims, was the brainchild of his great-great-great-grandfather, Joseph Peavey. My nephew, however, is not interested. My mother, nee Carson, rolls her eyes; she's heard this tale for more than forty years. My two brothers and cousin react as typical Yankees; they remain skeptical.

But I believe. I want to believe the story I heard my father tell when I was a kid, the one his father and grandfather had also told: that my many-times-great-grandfather Joseph Peavey emerged one day from the great North Woods with his new invention, but that, after an ill-advised detour for a little liquid refreshment, he ended up selling the patent for roughly $2.50 to the village smithy. Carried out west by pioneers, the peavey soon revolutionized the logging trade, and "peaveymen" came to be valued assets on any woods crew. To this day, the Bangor colossus, Paul Bunyan, holds a peavey in his stout grasp; Andrew Wyeth has immortalized the tool in his work as well. As for me, throughout my thirty-four years, this family story has afforded me the Victorian fantasy that I am a ruined heiress, a tale of woe which, if nothing else, comes in handy at cocktail parties when conversation lags.

Elizabeth Peavey

Some might say a peavey is not much to look at, but I find the one in my possession a thing of beauty: It has a 40-inch wooden shaft, worn smooth with age, and thirteen inches of red metal spike at its end. It is the fixed, levered hook, however, that attests to the true genius of Joe Peavey. The canthook, the log-rolling tool used by rivermen before the peavey's arrival, sported a hook as well, but one that was attached to an iron collar and moved about freely. To the uninitiated, the difference may seem slight. But to the river hogs of Joe Peavey's day, who nearly a century and a half ago scrambled across logs amid a river's tumultuous spring currents and risked their lives to free up the inevitable tangles and jams, it was the difference between working with a tool described as awkward and even dangerous, or working with a tool they could trust.

Not long ago I decided the time was ripe to clear up this family mystery, to distill the truth from the lore and the legend. My primary objective was nothing more than a big, fat "I told you so" and the smug complacence Aunt Dot and I could enjoy, ad infinitum, at future family gatherings. It wasn't as though I was ever going to head for the nearest North Woods logging camp to rub plaid-flannel elbows with a bunch of river hogs and wow them with tales of ancestral eminence. The closest this urban dweller gets to woods work is throwing another log on the fire, being quite convinced that she will contract Lyme disease if she strays too close to the woodpile. But, I decided, my precise relationship to Joe Peavey had simply become an ancestral itch that needed to be scratched. And if I happened to stumble upon an unclaimed fortune in the process, so be it.

My preliminary research was actually undertaken some fifteen years ago, when my parents and I stopped by the Peavey Memorial Library in Eastport. "You're looking for the logging Peaveys?" the librarian asked. "No, this library was built by the *grain* Peaveys, after they migrated to the Midwest and made their fortune." The news that one branch of the family had made good was heartening, but there seemed something vaguely evasive, even suspect, about the librarian's answer, which only added to the intrigue. Perhaps, I told myself, I was *twice* ruined.

My current, in-earnest research begins at the Portland Public Library. In the numerous logging books I consult, I find the story of the peavey to be as much Maine lore as it is family lore. All the books make some reference to Joe Peavey and his 1858 invention; many, in a school-marmish fashion, expurgate the drinking episode. The most colorful and complete description I find, however, is in Stewart Holbrook's *Holy Old Mackinaw.* His 1943 book recounts how one fine afternoon black-smith Joe Peavey was watching a crew of rivermen trying to break a log-jam with their "goddam so-and-so" swing canthooks. The "Big Idea"—to affix the levered hook—came to him, Holbrook tells us, "like a shaft of sudden sunlight." Joe Peavey jumped up, shouting a black-smith's equivalent of "Eureka!" He then hied on over to his Stillwater blacksmith shop and, with his son Daniel, banged and clanked out his modifications to the canthook.

All right, Holbrook has put me an inch closer to the truth, but not until I read the following passage do things begin to hum:

> So Joe Peavey made a drawing of it and set out on foot for Bangor and the post office, with the intention of getting it patented. On the way he stopped to see a blacksmith friend in Orono. Joe Peavey liked a glass of Medford rum, sometimes two glasses. His Orono friend poured liberally and Old Joe, his stomach warm, displayed the plans he was sending to the patent office. This called for another round of rum, and so on. When Joe awoke the next morning and shook the fog out of his old gray head, drawings and application for a 'patent cantdog,' not a peavey, were on their way to Washington, submitted by the Orono blacksmith.

So, according to Holbrook, the ruinous drinking incident is true; moreover, Joe was robbed of his patent! My chin lifts in regal disdain. My status of ruined heiress has now been elevated to *cheated,* ruined heiress. All I need now is to prove our undeniable connection. A call to Aunt Dot furnishes me with the names of my great-grandparents:

Wesley C. Peavey, of Swanville, and Mary Louise (Small) Peavey, who were wed in Jackson in 1876 and later buried in Monroe. Convinced the long-lost connection will present itself "like a shaft of sudden sunlight," I grab my DeLorme *Maine Atlas and Gazetteer* and hie north out of Portland. I envision myself uncovering a large, dusty tome buried in some distant town hall, its pages filled with the complete and illustrated Peavey family history. As I head up the highway, I rehearse my gloating proclamation for our next family gathering: "O, ye of little faith..." By now, anyone who has conducted genealogical research must be chortling at my naiveté.

Swanville, Monroe, and Jackson, all located within a few miles of each other northwest of Belfast, seem a perfect, bucolic backdrop to my developing melodrama. I first hit Swanville, one of those "don't-blink-or-you'll-miss-it" four corners. When I stop at the I.G.A. to get directions to the town hall, a pleasant gentleman informs me there is no town hall, but that the town clerk lives in the white farmhouse "just up over that hill, around the bend by the church, and down the road a piece on the left." Upon arrival, I find her home office to be crowded with people, desks, file cabinets, knickknacks, and stacks of papers. Country music blares from a portable radio. When my turn comes, she produces a document confirming my great-grandparents' marriage, but nothing more. I remain undaunted.

Time to forge on to my ancestral burial grounds in Monroe. In the brand-new town hall, I weave through a maze of sawhorses and boxes of books to the office of the town clerk. She does not know the name *Peavey*, but admits she's only lived in Monroe for fifty years, so she isn't really a local. She supplies me with directions to the town's eight cemeteries though, and I set out to do some tomb-stoning. The caretaker of one graveyard draws a rough hand over his white-stubbled chin and muses, "Peavey . . . Peavey." He then concludes, "Nope, I've been tending these graves a good many years and there's no Peaveys here." Wandering through the other cemeteries, I stumble upon but one lone

Peavey headstone. Protruding from the earth like a huge banged thumbnail, it states: "George E. Peavey." No date. No kin. No "Eureka!" No nothing.

So, it's off to Jackson. En route, the paved road gives way to gravel, and soon I'm lost. Fortunately, a road truck looms into sight, and the driver, with some hesitation, offers to squire me to Jackson. I bump along behind him in a trail of dust until he suddenly stops short. Climbing down out of his cab, he pushes back the brim of his hat and says with a smirk, "Well, here you are." If the other two towns were four corners, Jackson is, at best, two-and-a-half corners. There are a couple of barns and houses, a stretch of field, and a trailer with a sign advertising the sale of prostheses. The driver gives me a quizzical look. "Maybe you wanted Jackson *Corners*."

Back in Monroe, a helpful woman at the town hall tells me to check across the street at her husband's garage. "Anyone wants to know anything about Monroe," she says, "they ask Marshall." Deep in the oily interior of his shop, I state my case. When I mention the name *Peavey*, a smile creeps across his face. "Well," he says, "I never personally knew any of them, but I recall the name from listening to the old-timers reminisce." The Peaveys, it seems, made the smoothest moonshine in the whole county. While this bit of information fits into my boozy motif, I am no closer to fact. I now must bow to the ugly necessity of conducting real research. Somehow it had never occurred to me this project might actually entail work.

I next spend two arduous, head-aching, eye-burning days in Augusta, plowing through the files and stacks at the state library and poring over countless records and through reels of microfilm in the state archives. Finally, with the very able assistance of the librarians and archivists, I locate the record of my great-grandfather, Wesley C. Peavey: "died, 1912 in Monroe of internal injuries as a result of a fall, together with a weak heart; born, 1852 in Swanville to Sara/Sally Knowlton and Watson H./Henry W. Peavey/Pevey." (The name *Peavey* also appears as "Peavy," "Pevy," "Peevy," "Peva" and "Peveh.") I find that Wesley's parents were wed in 1847. I also discover the death record of Daniel Peavey, blacksmith, son of Joseph, who was born in Clinton in 1823 and died in Bangor in 1894. Here, I and my able assistants are stymied. It seems recordkeeping in the nineteenth century was, to say the least, spotty. Folks (my ancestors, in particular) apparently changed their names on caprice and moved around like nomads. To further complicate matters, I know so little about Joe Peavey that we can't begin to trace him.

During one of my frequent forays outside for fresh air, I notice a logging display in the Maine State Museum. I ask the guide if he has any biographical information on Peavey. He doesn't, but he offers to show me one of the log-rolling tools. I decline. For a month, I've been lugging my own peavey around in the back of my car like some sort of talisman, a misshapen dowser of truth, an auger of enlightenment—to no avail.

My final option is to plunge headlong into the heart of lumber country. Cheated inventor (and, apparently, bon vivant) Joe Peavey must've enjoyed a certain amount of notoriety, if not celebrity, in Victorian-age Bangor; surely there will be some documentation of his life at the Bangor Public Library. I slide open the oak file drawer with my genealogical fingers crossed, feeling a bit like Dorothy at the gates of Oz. And there it is: a card bearing Joe Peavey's name with the abbreviation "VF" penned on it. When I ask the librarian, she explains "VF" stands for "vertical file," with which she will presently return. Vertical file . . . this sounds fat and promising. Yet, when the files arrives, it is disappointingly slim. Still I am hopeful. I brace myself for that "shaft of sudden sunlight" but only find the same old information I already know. All that's new are Joe's birth date (1799) and death date (1873); and that, in addition to Daniel, Joe had another son, Ira. The file also notes brightly: "Joe Peavey, inventor of the cantdog."

Across town at the Bangor Historical Society, a portrait of Joe shows an old man sitting regally upon a heavy wooden chair with an inquisitive pooch at his side. The only family resemblance I can draw is that his thick black boots resemble the Doc Martens I am sporting. Then the boom falls. Leaning forward in a conspiratorial manner, the historian tells me, "We don't actually have any proof that this is Joe Peavey. That's only what we were told by the portrait's donors."

My pilgrimage north would not be complete without a visit to the factory-sawmill that bears my name, the Peavey Manufacturing Company in Eddington. There, I am shown the old Joe Peavey portrait and also a picture of a younger Joe Peavey—somewhat resembling Bruce Springsteen in a 10-gallon hat—taken in 1857 with the future inventor leaning jauntily on a pre-peavey canthook. Patent or no, Peavey's descendants founded the company to produce Joe's invention and, as owner Debbie Buswell explains, it still makes peaveys, as well as other woods and construction tools. While there are plenty of peaveys to be seen at Peavey Manufacturing, there's not a Peavey to be found. It's all Buswells and Delanos now. The Peaveys lie buried in Bangor's Mount Hope Cemetery, under a stone adorned with carved peaveys.

On my way home, I make one last stop at the state archives, but even with my new information, no connection—or non-connection—to Joe can be found. Glancing around at the glazed-eyed genealogists glued to their microfilm screens, I ask the man at the desk if people actually research their family trees for pleasure. He shrugs. "Only the masochists."

Back home, I call Aunt Dot with my inconclusive findings. She is silent for a moment. "Well, I've heard the story all my life," she says at last. "From my father and from my grandmother—she wasn't even a Peavey, so she was bamboozled, too." I gaze at the photocopied pictures of Old Joe before me and he returns a stern glare. For a moment, I imagine I can hear his voice, saying: "Quit yer bellyachin' and get on with it. Life's for the living."

Well, then, if my ancestors were not inventors of tools, then they were certainly inventors of tales. "So," I reason with my aunt over the phone, "if I can't prove we're not related, then the story could be true—if we believe it." And then, just before I hang up, another thought occurs to me. "Aunt Dot," I say, grasping at straws, "do you recall hearing anything about the *grain* Peaveys?"

Might as well go for the whole shootin' match.

[1993]

Remembrance of Meals Past

Nestled in a capacious forest-green banquette at the Pilots Grill in Bangor, I watch the tines of my fork slide into the homemade strawberry cheesecake before me and am cast into a Proustian reverie. I have not ordered this favorite dessert of my youth since my college days. But a visit to this famed Bangor dinner house has stirred a remembrance of meals past—of seam-splitting dinners out with my parents, in which I stuffed myself to make up for the dietary blight of cafeteria food. Never a shy child when it came to my wants, I recall that I grew uncharacteristically timid with my parents the minute a linen napkin and a giant menu were placed on my lap. "Have the shrimp cocktail," my father would urge. "Have the large steak," my mother would insist. "You'll still have room for cheesecake." My protests were always small, my appetite—as we Yankees like to say—healthy. There was always room for more.

It is not just the cheesecake that has inspired these thoughts. The Pilots Grill, a Bangor institution for over fifty years and the area's oldest family-run restaurant, has a timeless feel. Located in a commercial district on Route 2 on the outskirts of the city, the restaurant is housed in a sprawling, low-slung structure, featuring an angular, '60s-style, carport at its entrance. You know the minute you enter through the glass doors into the darkened foyer, you are not in for some nouvelley dining experience. Smells of coffee, French fries, and grilled steak waft from the dining room, instantly signaling that a no-nonsense, good meal awaits you. And simple comfort food is precisely what the Pilots Grill is all about.

Started as a luncheon counter at the Bangor Airport by the Zoidis family in 1940, the Pilots Grill remains a family operation. The business is currently run by William Zoidis and his daughter Paulette, who left Corporate America two years ago to help run her father's restaurant. And the Pilots Grill extended family runs beyond kin. The restaurant has employed only two sets of chefs since its opening. Moreover, several members of the wait staff could be termed "lifers," some with as many as twenty-five and thirty years of service logged on their sturdy shoes. But perhaps the real test of the restaurant's extended family is its clientele, who could also be said to be lifers. Airline employees (and, yes, pilots) remain tried and true patrons, along with an abundance of Bangorites, who have made dining at the Grill their own family tradition. Paulette says that when people call to make a reservation, they not only know what room they wish to sit in, they also know the number of the booth they desire.

And there are plenty of options. The Pilots Grill in 1997 is a crazy mix of pieced-together rooms, two of which—the cozy, paneled Knotty Pine Room and the Sky View Room (so named for its expansive windows, from which diners could once watch airport activity)—were moved from the airport to the present location in 1957, when a major runway expansion paved over the restaurant's original site. To these two original rooms were added a 180-person banquet room, an additional dining room, and a lounge (formerly a gift shop and now a bistro) to make up what is today's Pilots Grill.

Once you've selected where you wish to be seated, you are then confronted with the problem of what to eat. The vast menu is almost infinitely accommodating, offering selections to meet not only every palate and budget, but also every dietary need. There is the traditional array of steaks, chops, and seafood (the Pilots Grill "famous" house steaks are hand-cut on the premises, the seafood is the freshest available, and local produce is used whenever possible), but there is also a nod to contemporary eating trends: Paulette has introduced brick-oven pizza to the bistro, and the regular menu features a number of low-fat items, any of which can be prepared for particular dietary restrictions.

But not for me, thanks. Dwarfed in my banquette, I feel eighteen again—and I'm hungry. With nobody's urging, I start with the shrimp cocktail, which is served in a veritable pyramid of glass and china. The jumbo shrimp are slung over a cocktail glass, which is sunk in a crockery bowl of ice, which sits atop a liner, which is served upon a plate. This, I think, is not a food item, it's an event. As it should be—and always used to be. Prior to the appetizer's arrival, while I am still mulling over the menu, a basket of crackers, topped with a big, soft disk of a roll, and a serving of the Grill's famous cheese dip is placed before me. (The cheese dip, which was created to lure customers into the restaurant's lounge when it was first opened in the 1950s, has gained such repute over the years, it is now being sold in grocery stores, as is Pilots Grill's popular Greek salad dressing.) I pick and sample, peruse the menu and then, following my gustative memory track, order the—not large, but ample—10-ounce steak. With fries.

My waitress, over the course of my meal, neither hovers nor forsakes me. My expansive order is taken at leisure. When the plates begin mounting at an alarming rate, she offers to remove a few, but when I scrunch up my shoulders and say I might like to hold onto my salad for another minute, she smiles broadly and nods, as if to say, "That's right, you eat. You don't know when you'll get your next good meal." I want to throw my arms around her waist, bury my head in her apron, and sob, "How did you know this is the sort of place my parents always took me when they thought I was starving at school?", but continue eating instead.

All around me, diners seem to be in a similar swoon. Elders are supping on New England boiled dinners, businessmen are carving into steaks, matrons dally over fancy sandwich plates, tots are twirling spaghetti. Manhattans and martinis drift by on trays as though this were the Eisenhower era. There's not a bottle of mineral water or a leaf of radicchio in sight.

My seams are indeed splitting when I request coffee and the check. That broad smile again spreads across my waitress's face. "You're not going to go without a piece of pie. They're made right here every day by one of our waitresses." I have already gone overboard. The sensible grown-up in me raises a hand, but my waitress detects the falseness of this gesture. "You should at least hear what they are." She lists them off. My resolve weakens. "What would *you* have?", I ask, prodding her to insist. Her eyes drift heavenward. "I just can't resist our cheesecake," she says, as though reading my mind.

It has been said the only real pleasure on this earth is in pleasure's anticipation, but I don't know. I am genuinely happy as I savor that first bite of cheesecake after these many years. And then, as I glance across the room, I see a young woman—probably college age—dining with her parents. Her eyes, with their lean and hungry look, dart around the menu. I want to rush over and tell her to enjoy herself, to go ahead and have the shrimp cocktail, to say that a meal like this might not ever taste so good again.

But then that would mean tearing myself away from my dessert. And, besides, after this visit to the Pilots Grill, I'm not so sure I could utter that statement with much conviction.

[1997]

Laying Claim to Monhegan

Mention Monhegan Island at an arty Manhattan gathering, and you are more likely to get knowing nods from the urbanites than from many Maine residents. Sure, Mainers know of Monhegan, but it tends to be one of those places locals intend to see rather than actually visit.

I must confess I was one of those Mainers, until I visited the island a couple of years ago with my mother. We strolled through the woods and out to the cliffs, lounged on the rocker-lined porch of the Monhegan House, meandered through the village and its artist studios, and watched deer gather in a clearing at dusk. I was charmed. We returned the following year for more of the same. These were restful, enjoyable overnights, yet something was lacking. Yes, I had now been to the fabled island, but I had laid no claim to it. I felt this was a chunk of Maine that would not yield to me, and being mildly possessive about my home state, I decided there was but one thing to do: take the island for my own.

Judging from prior visits, there were limited ways to do this. I could become a year-round resident (not terribly convenient); I could insinuate myself into the close-knit summer community and get an invitation for an extended stay in one of their cottages (not likely); I could bum a paintbrush and canvas from one of my artist friends and plant an easel seaside with the other dabblers (not a chance); or I could tackle the island for the wild and rocky landmass that it is (apparently my only alternative).

Monhegan Island, roughly ten miles off the Maine coast, is best known as an artist colony. Anyone with the slightest interest in American painting must have at least a rough picture of it in their mind's eye from the works of artists—Rockwell Kent, Robert Henri, George Bellows, Edward Hopper, Marsden Hartley, Abraham Bogdanove and others—who have immortalized its rugged coast and inland forests since the early part of the century. In terms of contemporary painters—both budding and established—you can hardly swing an easel on the island without clubbing one upside the head. But Monhegan also offers some of the most heart-pounding (in terms of both beauty and rigor) hiking trails in the state. And it is toward this aspect of the island I turn my sights.

In preparation for the trip, I scan a couple hiking guides concerning the seventeen miles of trails that cross and circumscribe the 700-acre island. I have but one goal in mind, and that is to circle the island's outer trail . . . lasso Monhegan, as it were. I am warned of the possibility of dangerous falls into the sea and that rescue would be unlikely. (The Monhegan Association trail map further cautions that tidal currents and undertow make rescue "impossible.") Not that I plan to dance along any cliff ledge and not that I'm a scaredy-cat, but I decide a traveling companion is in order, and I prevail upon a friend—one of those Monhegan-free Mainers—to join me for a jaunt around the island. Just in case.

As our ferry rounds Manana Island—an uninhabited hunk of rock that directly faces Monhegan, a mere 150 yards across the harbor—and we approach our destination, the island seems benign. Weathered shake-shingle cottages with green or white trim cluster around the eastern shore. The island's gray lighthouse stands on a high slope over the village. Boats gently rock in the sheltered harbor. But I have seen the sheer cliffs that fall away down into the sea on the island's other side and know this serene façade is deceptive.

Glancing around the ferry, I note my fellow travelers do not appear to be especially outdoorsy looking. I see sandals and sneakers. I see women with painted nails and retirees sporting fanny packs. New York accents rise above the din of the ferry's engine. These are not people who have come to take the island as I have. I have gear. I have a plan. Already, I feel my smugness growing.

From the moment we set foot on Monhegan, time distorts; it is at once ample and precious. An overnight affords us a full afternoon and the following morning for exploring the island's trails, but I'm here on a mission. My very persuasive slacker side whispers, "Relax." But then there is the voice in the back of my brain that barks, "Go!"

In the end, both sides win. Because on Monhegan, no matter how hard you try, rushing is impossible. Debarking the ferry, we load our baggage onto the back of a dilapidated pickup truck, which is backed up to the dock and sports a crudely painted "Monhegan House" sign. A leisurely stroll through the village takes us to the hotel. After checking in, I am anxious to hit the trail, but decide perhaps a glance at the map and a sit on the porch is first in order. Besides, from our perch, which faces the Monhegan Store and the post office, and is en route to many of the trail heads, we get to take in all the action. If you want to get an impression of the island's population on any given day, this is the place to plant yourself.

There is a decided caste system on the island. Day-trippers are on the lowest rung of the hierarchy, just a bit lower than overnight guests. (We get a porch to stake out, after all.) Next are the visiting painters, who stalk the grounds with wooden easels strapped to their backs and who stop to compliment each other about works in progress. Crowding the top are the summer residents, scooting around in their golf carts, stopping at the store for gallons of bottled water, gabbing outside the post office, shouting greetings as they pass on the village's dirt road.

These people rarely make eye contact with those at the bottom of the caste level. If you have been given a passing smile, you can bet it was from one of your ilk. There is a feeling that the summer people don't tolerate us interlopers so much as merely choose not to see us. Year-round residents are truly the ones who own the island, however, and as they rattle by in their rusted-out trucks, bumpers held on with rope and twine, they seem to take it all with just a bit of wry humor and distance.

But once you leave the confines of the village, the caste system falls away. Out on the trails the voices dim, the hubbub dies down, golf carts are useless, and you discover what the island's real appeal is: its rugged beauty, its often fierce terrain, and its vast expanse of surrounding sea. People who venture out are judged by their mettle. Did you wear proper shoes? Do you have food and water? Did you bring your map? Are you prepared to dig your nails into rock face? These are the things that count, and these are the things I am here for.

Lobster Cove Road leads us up a gentle grade, past a number of summer homes and studios, to the southern tip of the island—a flattened, jagged point. I have been here before and am anxious to get the show on the road, but my hiking companion is not. I make myself understand that I have to calm my aggressive instincts, to take the island walk not as a thing to be conquered but as something to be savored. Thus, we meander and poke around the shore, examine the tidal pools, gawk at Jamie Wyeth's house, scramble over the rocks, and investigate the rusted carcass of the *D. T. Sheridan,* a 110-foot coal vessel that was shipwrecked in 1948. Eventually, we plod on.

A fairly steep slope brings us next to Burnt Head, where a number of picnickers lounge and painters stand at easels along the cliff head. This is one of the more popular points on the island, easily accessible by two inland trails. Below us, the Coke-bottle-green water churns. Gulls arc overhead. We have covered ground, but have not yet broken from the fray.

We forge north on the outside Cliff Trail, which winds in and out of woodlands. The air is vibrant with pine and salt; the sound of the sea at once roars and then silences. Our pipes start working. We realize early on, this is no walk in the park. As we make our way toward the guano-stained Gull Cove and its limpid, algeaed pool, we are already breaking a sweat. A layer of clothing comes off. Consulting the map—on which difficult sections of the trail are marked by a jagged line that looks like a series of Ws—we see that only a few of these Ws have been traversed, with many more to come. Our hike has hardly begun.

A man with a dachshund blasts by us for a second time. Our accidental traveling companions are determined from the git-go, because only an idiot with a mission (me) would try to make a race out of hiking around this island without pausing often along the way. The sensible traveler (and I rather quickly become sensible) knows to take this route at leisure. We share our hike therefore with the dachshund man, a lone woman in a blaze-orange anorak, and a young couple we pass and are passed by numerous times along the way. The dachshund man and anorak woman do not speak or even make eye contact with us; the young couple is inclined to chat. "So how's it going?" they merrily ask, as they rest midway up a particularly steep ledge. I smirk, but we are toiling and disinclined to speak. Air, at this point, is a valuable commodity.

Each turn on our perambulation of the island offers another challenge, whether it be hopscotching across the thatch of thick roots that cross our path or navigating the sudden and vertigo-inducing ledges we have to climb with knee and fist against rock, or just working to keep ourselves on course. While the trails are well-marked, it is not difficult to miss the cairns and small markers and wander astray. We make a couple of wrong turns, dead-end once or twice, but never get seriously lost as we scale White Head, Little White Head, traverse Squeaker Cove, and make the bold ascent to Blackhead (many, many Ws).

My mother has told me that only horses sweat and that ladies get dewy. If I am not sweating, then I am at least dewy to the nth degree. We stop on a windswept ledge on the crest of Black Head and picnic on sourdough baguette and strawberry-rhubarb jam (purchased from the tony provisions shop in the village) and fruit and cheese brought from home. As we lounge in the sun, we spot five dolphins frolicking offshore. My conquistador heart has come to rest.

Soon, we will wend our way off our crest, down to the woody trail to Pulpit Rock, and around the north point past Pebble Beach, where the young couple is now beachcombing. They look up—this time without words, but with knowing glances—and we smile back. They know what we know: that we have now laid a particular claim to Monhegan. At last, I feel the island is mine.

As the trail leads us past the fisherfolks' homes and back into the village, a golf cart trundles toward us. We make our way past it, en route back to the hotel, where we know two rockers on our porch await.

Call me a snob, but I do not even give the driver a glance.

[1998]

Easy as π

Something smells funny. It's an acrid, just-turned-the-heat-on-in-an-ancient-high-school-gym odor, and it makes my eyes burn. This is not a good sign, since I have yet to open the bag of flour or crack that tin of shortening. These and other ingredients are lined on the kitchen counter in military order. I do not take the task before me lightly. I am about to bake my first pie. A blueberry pie.

Let me start by saying I am no cook. I have never put up a pickle, mashed a potato, or roasted a leg of mutton. On the rare occasions a meal has been required of me, disaster of some sort has struck. For example, I once tried to serve poached eggs on English muffins to houseguests. After my friends decided I had been in the kitchen for an inordinate amount of time for so small a task, they crept around the corner to find eggs boiled dry, muffins burnt to hockey pucks, and me, standing at the window, hands clasped behind my back, with all the gravity of a captain about to go down with her ship.

See, in my tomboyish youth, I thought learning practical arts like cooking or typing was a waste of my talents—an unfortunate judgment call, considering how much time I now spend at a keyboard or groaning board each day.

Noncooking was fine in youth, but in adult life my culinary

deficiencies started to become a social handicap. The mere question "Had dinner at Peavey's recently?" was enough to send friends and family into gales of laughter. I was forty and newly married. It was time for a change. "I'll show 'em," I thought. "I'll bake a blueberry pie."

Why pie? Because as Maine author John Gould tells us in his book *Farmer Takes A Wife,* "there's no excuse for being without pie." Blueberry pie has been a staple of Maine cooking for time immemorial, as basic as boiled lobster or fish stew, and if I were to call myself a proper Yankee bride, pie-making must be learned. Besides, a friend had dared me.

The endeavor required research. I began with the grande dame of Maine cooking, Marjorie Standish. I felt assured she would guide me and hold my hand through the operation, yet when I checked for blueberry pie in the index of one of her cookbooks, I discovered she only offered instruction on how to freeze a blueberry pie, which I interpreted to mean that every Maine cook worth her Bean boots was just born knowing how to make a blueberry pie, a gene this native was quite clearly lacking.

But there were other resources—relatives, friends, books, magazine articles—ready to help. Everyone but me, it seemed, was a pie expert. What I learned is that pie is all about crust, and crust is all about technique. This would've been all well and good if there were just one technique. But I also learned there are myriad methodologies, which left the uninitiated (me) adrift in this cooking business. Winging it was in order.

I consulted all of my cookbooks—both of them—and checked my larder for the necessary ingredients: flour (no), sugar (in stolen restaurant packets only), lard (no), butter (no), tapioca (yeah, whatever), cold water, and salt (yes!), and made my grocery list. In terms of equipment, I came up equally as short. As luck would have it, however, my new husband—an able pie man—had brought to our marriage pie plates, a sifter, generous mixing bowls, and a rolling pin. The only thing remaining was the acquisition of berries.

It was high blueberry season, and I could have bought them at the grocery store. I could've found a good roadside stand, but if this was going to be my pie, I would harvest the fruit myself. Dammit.

So, I imposed upon my sister-in-law, who has two berry bushes in her yard. I borrowed a stained cardboard carton and went at the chore. Plunk, plunk. I had not picked blueberries since I was a child, and the memory was much sweeter than the act. Plunk, plunk, plunk. I could still see the bottom of the carton. The bush sparkled with coupling Japanese beetles. It looked like a woman had clipped her earrings to the branches. I wondered if I could contract coupling-Japanese-beetle-berry disease from this bush. The sun dazzled. Plunk, plunk. The dalmatian, Watson, joined me. Spreading his lips in the fakest smile you've ever seen on a mutt, he tenderly plucked the most savory berries, one at a time. My arms and legs ached. I sat down and tore clumps of leaves and berries and tossed them into the box. By the end, I was on my back, plucking one berry at a time. I was hot. I was tired. I decided I wouldn't make a very good homesteader.

Still, I had enough berries for pie, and I returned home with my fragile cargo poised daintily on the passenger seat. I would go to bed early, I decided, because the next day was going to be Pie Day and I wanted to be sharp.

The moment I opened my eyes, however, my mood darkened. Before me was one of those singular Maine summer days—achingly blue sky, just a bit of breeze. Was I going boating? Was I going swimming? Was I going for a stomp in the woods? No. I was being banished to my kitchen to cook. To bake. I felt like I was being punished.

And that is how I arrived at this moment in this smelly kitchen, where the awful odor only adds to my misery. Then I realize that in my zeal to get the pie over with as soon as possible, by turning on the oven to preheat, I have caused a small brush fire in the stove and am smelling the hot stench of disuse, roasting dust bunnies, and broiled cobwebs.

I quickly turn the stove off. I am not quite ready for that part of the operation anyway. My husband, who has already told me he doesn't want to miss this adventure, waltzes into the kitchen and is opening the flour and starting in on the pie advice. I am trying to collect my pie-baking thoughts, and he is cramping my style. The hand goes up, and he is sent from the kitchen.

Okay, first. Sift flour. I dump in a cup and it drifts to the bottom of the giant blue crockery mixing bowl. Salt and more flour follow. That's not too hard. Next, however, is the dreaded Adding of the Lard. Lard, it seems, is a large bone of contention among those who bake pies. Some insist on the real thing, and I'm sure Martha Stewart types would suggest you render it yourself. Some want a blend of butter and lard, margarine and butter, straight shortening, or a combination of these. I have (with the counsel of my pie man) opted for a shortening-butter combination. One of my cookbooks tells me all the ingredients should be 70 degrees; the other says they should all be very cold. Because the shortening was left on the counter and the butter in the refrigerator, I decide to split the difference. I measure out the shortening and then smoosh (a technical cooking term) the butter in the measuring cup. The cold butter does not take well to the pliant shortening, but I smash it down as best I can. The small chips of yellow make a festive mosaic on the white background, but do not look baking-friendly.

Now it's time to introduce the lard to the dry ingredients. Second in controversy only to the choice of lard is the way it is added to the mix. One might use a pastry cutter (if one owned a pastry cutter), knives, or fingertips. My pie man recommends an electric mixer. I decide to try cutting the lard in with two knives, because I believe this is how my mother did it. I recall some important figure in my life going at dough with two knives, although I may have seen the act on a cooking show on TV.

Click, click, click go the knives as I work them as though untossing a salad. The shortening-butter combo remains gummed to one side of the bowl, and the flour flies freely over the edge. My cookbook tells me I should continue until the mixture has the grain of cornmeal. I look down at the lightly coated, flat, gummy bits of white and yellow and decide to break out the mixer and give it a spin or two around the bowl. Finally, I pick up the bits and roll them between my fingers until they semi-dissolve. A glance back at the general comments on crust in *Joy of Cooking* tells me I should've been handling my dough lightly. Oh, well.

Next I ready my rolling area with an economical dusting of flour—economical, because I am told too much added flour will make my crust tough. Tough crust is to be pitied and is the downfall of many a pie. My dough-mauling has already retarded the development of my glutens according to the book; I will not over-flour.

I take my dusted rolling pin to the lump of dough, starting from the center of the blob and working my way out. The dough squishes and sticks to the rolling pin. I flour it again and give the dough another workout. A trickle of sweat rolls down my back. The blob flattens and sprawls. I am running out of counter space.

I decide it's time to get this crust in the pie pan, and I turn the oven back on. Smarty-pants *Joy of Cooking* tells me: "It's a poor pie crust that requires a greased pan." To grease is to give up and admit defeat. Not to grease runs the risk of my pie welding to the pan. I figure the extra grease will even out all the flour I've added to the rolling pin and opt for a heavy coating.

Now comes the ceremonial Lifting of the Crust. There are two style options: fold it in half and lift it into the pan or roll the edge around the pin and roll it up like a giant, floury, greasy paper towel. Instead, I just try to pick the thing up. But it's glued to the counter. I get a spatula. The dough starts to tear. I finally get the now-ragged thing in my hands and drop it in the pan.

Sad. I am utterly sad.

I stomp out of the kitchen, past my husband, and plop down on the front stoop. He follows me. "I wrecked it," I pout. He says we'll go fix it. I don't want to. I want to stay outside. I don't want to be a cook. I don't want to make pie. But finally I give in. I have too much invested.

I am heartened by the repairs my husband makes to the torn crust and by the beautiful berries that become a purple stew when the sugar, tapioca, and cinnamon are added. I spoon the goo (another technical cooking term) into the pie crust, flop down the top crust, and go at the edges with a knife. Then, the final touch: the pinching of the crust with the thumb and forefinger to make that attractive edge. Only problem is, I have cut away all the pinchable parts and have to squeeze the two crusts together and kind of roll the edge down. I add a few knife slits to the sizable tear in the upper crust, put the thing in the well-preheated oven, and throw myself on the couch for a post-pie swoon.

At the appointed hour, my husband and I gather around the stove to take the pie out of the oven. The crust is lightly browned, looking neither tough nor chewy. The thick purple berry juice bubbles around the edges—a good sign according to my pie man. We stand and gaze down at the thing in a moment of awe. My pie is done. *My* pie.

Suddenly, I long for an inviting windowsill on which to let it cool. I long to shoo away mischievous neighborhood youths with my apron: "Now you boys get away from there. That pie's not for you." I long to flaunt this pie before my friend who made the dare. I long for a church supper, a bake sale, a family dinner, so someone could ask what I brought and I could smugly say, "pie."

But there are none of these opportunities. There are only the two of us, and the two of us will sit down in the blue twilight of this coming summer evening, as couples have sat down to countless blue twilit Maine evenings for generations, and top off supper with blueberry pie. And the pie will be fine.

Yes, Mr. Gould, there should always be pie.

[2000]

Hog-Wild for Hog Island

As I pack for my stay at the National Audubon's Field Ecology Workshop on Hog Island, located off the midcoast town of Bremen, I am as nervous and excited as a kid preparing for her first sleep-away camp. What will my bunkmates be like? Will my binoculars pass muster? Will we make potholders from kelp? Will one of the more experienced campers kick slime mold in my face? The last concern is not an actual one: I do not know that slime mold even exists until I attend the camp's fungi workshop.

You see, I am something of *a poseur* naturalist. Although I spend a good amount of time in Maine's great outdoors, my identification skills concerning its flora and fauna have been limited to the occasional imaginative utterance—"brown-belted bob-o-link" or "tri-tasseled tamarack" —while afield. That I frequently make my forays with people as unscientific as I, has helped perpetuate my ruse. But now I am about to attend a camp designed for those in the know. The jig's up.

Ponchoed and slickered campers arrive in fits and starts at the dock at the Todd Wildlife Sanctuary in the teeming rain. We are handed nametags, which will remain slung around our necks all week, and wait in a low boathouse to make the quarter-mile voyage over to the island. To help break the ice, one of the instructors waxes rhapsodic about the food. "They don't call it Hog Island for nothing," she says.

When the *Puffin IV* lands at the island, we have a bit of time to get settled before we are swept up in the whirlwind schedule that will fill our days. Campers are housed in one of three rustic buildings: the recently refurbished Queen Mary Suite, perched at the water's edge and located above the marine lab; the Port Hole, a two-story dorm with semi-private rooms; and my home for the next few days, the all-female Crow's Nest, a campy bunkhouse located down a fir- and fern-lined pathway that hugs a small rocky beach. The great central room is lined with lumpy cots piled with mismatched linens. "The Crow's Nest is fun," says Wendy, another of the camp's instructors, who has escorted us to our digs. This blonde and cheerful marine biologist has the exuberance of a camp councilor. I'm relieved she doesn't spirit us away for a romping volleyball game. No, that will be later in the week.

As I smooth out sheets on my chosen bunk, there's a quick knock on the screen door and a voice calls, "Man on deck!" as a student assistant hauls in another load of dripping luggage and dumps it on the floor. The rain has ebbed. I stow my gear and head back to the action.

A crowd has gathered in the dining room, where the island's chef, John "Yanni" Laberge, has laid out a welcoming spread: clam chowder, olives, nuts, crumbly cookies. A line snakes at the coffee urn; the screen door bangs as people mill in and out. Conversation is at a murmur; those who traveled together—married couples, friends, cousins—for now keep mostly to themselves. The majority of these campers are nearing or beyond retirement age; women way outnumber men; and most, I will learn over the week, are educators of one sort or another, from as far west as Oklahoma, as far south as Florida, and with major concentrations from New York and the Midwest. Many are here on scholarships. I am the sole Mainer, and, I suspect, the sole novice.

The dining room is located in the Bridge, a 19th-century farmhouse that harks back to the early history of Hog Island. The first question is, of course, how such a lovely island acquired such a homely name. The answer is simple: The islands in Muscongus Bay were used for farming in the 1800s, and hogs were once kept on the island. Farming gradually ceded to leisure, and around the turn of the century, the 30-acre peninsula that juts off the north end of this 330-acre island served as a summer resort for vacationing urban ladies, who were reported to have sipped mint juleps on the site where algae is now probed under a microscope in the island lab.

Then, in 1908, Mabel Loomis Todd, a summer visitor from Amherst, Massachusetts, set to work to acquire the entire island—whose mature spruce woods were in danger of being razed—and preserve it as a wildlife sanctuary. The process was slow. Upon her death, her daughter, Millicent Todd Bingham, took up the task. She envisioned a nature camp. Parcel by parcel, the island was purchased, and it was turned over to the National Audubon Society in 1935. The next year, the first Nature Camp for Adult Leaders opened, with none other than Roger Tory Peterson, Himself, as the camp's director. Since then, Audubon programs have been offered every year, aside for two summers during World War II. The schedule now includes youth and family camps, ones focused on photography, sea kayaking, birding, or ecology. The island is not open to the general public.

I wander down to the rocky beach as I wait for our first workshop to begin. The shoreline is at once familiar and enigmatic. I have been looking at vistas like this all my life, but it occurs to me I know little about them. As I make my way back, Steve, a man carting a spotting scope and impressive camera mounted on a self-styled wooden gunstock-like apparatus, asks me in his Long Island accent if I have spotted anything. I say a seal, an osprey, a cormorant, trying to sound knowledgeable. When he asks, "D.C.?", I hear "Geesies." "No, no geesies," I say. He gives me a look and then says, "I said D.C.—double-breasted cormorant." Already I know I am over my head.

A resounding land-mounted bell signals five minutes till meteorology class. The bell gongs five minutes prior to all workshops, outings, and meals. We learn to move to the sound of the bell. This may be summer camp for adults, but the same rites and rituals of youth camp prevail.

At dinner, we sit at tables of eight, dining family-style. Great bowls, covered tureens, are retrieved by each table's runner. Over the week, we feast on fresh fish, fruits and vegetables, salads, heaps of pasta and beans, homemade soups and granola, freshly baked breads, and desserts spangled with berries. Chef Yanni is a god on the island and renowned up and down the nearby Pemaquid Peninsula. With sparkling eyes, balding pate, and purple-painted toenails, he emerges from the kitchen to elaborate on each meal's menu. We listen reverently and feed like lumberjacks.

After an orientation in the Fish House, the island's library and conference center, a group of us make our way out to a point and sprawl on the rocks for an astronomy talk by Rick Ylagan, a youthful and energetic Bangor High School teacher who is celebrating his tenth year as an instructor on Hog Island. A blood-orange moon slides up over the horizon. We pick out stars and constellations and try to stay awake.

The next morning, my alarm goes off at 5:30. My eyes are gummed shut. It's another hour till the wake-up bell, but a number of us are trying to make it to the 6 A.M. bird walk. I stumble out of the Crow's Nest with another woman who seems just a little too chipper for that hour. "This is great," she says. "I have no kids to feed, no job to go to. I could do this forever."

At first, the rigorous schedule and the strains of communal living turn many of us into automatons, but within a day or two everyone seems to acclimate. I spring out of bed before six each morning to attend a bird walk or just roam around the island. As the week progresses, guards come down and the din of conversation at meals and activities rises. One afternoon I receive a jolly slap on the back by a fellow camper when I refer to a clam-in-hand as a biped. He nearly winds me.

Each day, we are given a selection of morning, afternoon, and evening workshops and activities from which to choose: botany, marine biology, geology, birding, journaling. There are excursions: a canoe trip on the Pemaquid River; a bird walk in the mainland village of Medomak; a visit to Eastern Egg Rock, where Dr. Stephen Kress started his famed Puffin Project, Kress visits the camp to address us one night, and when he speaks, the reverence in the room is palpable. He is the Tom Jones of the birding world, and for one brief instant I fear the speaker might be pelted with undergarments from his appreciative audience.

My notebook gradually fills with notations and childish sketches. I learn to key out ferns and conifers and identify eskers and drumlins. I wade into tidal pools, while my more learned friends probe algae, pluck out eel fish and sculpin, and discuss the complex sex life of rockweed. I listen as the birders "pish" for warblers or point out the distinctive (to their ears, not mine) calls: "please, please, pleased to meetcha"s, "zee zazz zo zo zee"s and "witchity witchities." It is as though a veneer on my Maine world has been peeled back, and I can, for the first time, see of what it's really made. Even in all this activity, there is an air of wonder among the campers, who see Maine as a sacred place. Their awe of my home pleases me.

Barbara Levin, an older woman from Long Island, with soft blonde curls, has been coming to Hog Island for years. She's the camp's first full-time volunteer, runs the gift shop, and is anxious to share her affection for the island: "It's not so much learning the names of things or spotting birds that make this experience so special," she says, almost dreamily. "It's the people, and it's the island itself."

Sam Hands, the director of the camp, agrees. Although he admits the camp is designed to educate and send a strong message of conservation—one that, with hope, will trickle down to these teachers' students—he knows the experience has more resonance. "It means a lot for people to form bonds with people who share the same beliefs," he says.

And they are right. Within a few days, the members of our camp have become comrades. Groups splinter off and friendships are formed. There's John, who patiently answers my endless questions all week; Erica, with whom I discuss life and work over coffee in the mosquito-ridden twilight; Margie, my bunkmate, with whom I perform surgery on the Crow's Nest's running toilet one midnight; and my best camp buddy, Kate, an expatriated Mainer now living in Oklahoma, who gets weepy when I depart. I survive a mismapped trek through the woods with a woman named Dorothy and emerge with bramble scratches on my legs, two bowties of ferns springing from my hiking boots, a list of required reading, and a new friend.

I feel I have been given the chance to make up for all the science classes I dozed through over my schooling, with fifty concerned and excited teachers at my ready. Yes, I can now identify a chestnut-sided warbler (sort of) and discern between a red and white spruce almost instantly, but what I really take from the island is the connection I have made with these people who care passionately for the natural world and who are generous with their knowledge—and further, a greater appreciation for the environment and the state in which I live. A week on Hog Island is exotic for those from away. For Mainers, it's required learning.

And so, if, on some future hiking trip, I gesture to a plant and say, "bastard toad flax," it will not be without a smug smile. I happen to know what it really is. I've been taught by the best.

[1999]

Bingo Weenie

It never once occurs to me that I am not going to win. Not when I make my reservation a week in advance. Not as I embark on the two plus-hour drive on the appointed day. Not even as I am waved into one of the few remaining parking spots in the nearly filled-to-capacity lot. Hell, I haven't even bothered to wear my lucky socks.

I have come to play high-stakes bingo at the Penobscot Indian's Sockalexis Bingo Palace on Indian Island, just outside of Old Town, and I believe with every fiber of my bingo being that I am going to walk away a winner.

Okay, so I've never played bingo before—let alone high stakes bingo—but I reason that someone has to win. I'm a fairly nice person. I could use one of those $25,000 jackpots. Why not me?

But it's not just the lure of cash that drives my quest. The whole bingo phenomenon has always been something of a mystery to me. I've wondered what really goes on in those church basements and bingo parlors. Who plays? Is it just the domain of little old ladies, or do thick-necked guys with pinkie rings also compete? And just what is the allure of this game that drives Mainers to obsession? I figure a day of Penobscot High Stakes Bingo, Maine's ultimate bingo tourney, which takes place roughly every two months, is the best way to find out. And if I can earn a little dough in the process, all the better.

Elizabeth Peavey

When I made my reservation, I was informed that regular play starts at 12:30 P.M., with an hour of "warm-ups" beforehand. I thought 11 A.M. would be a respectable arrival time—that is, until now, as I walk by bus after bus bearing plates from Newfoundland, New York, Nova Scotia, Rhode Island, Connecticut, Massachusetts, and Vermont, and enter the great hall. I stand at the doors and take in the sea of people before me. While the crowd clearly favors the female senior set, there are also working stiffs, young moms, and a smattering of college-age men and women. Demographics aside, all of these players have one thing in common: they are utterly ensconced. Coolers are stashed under the tables. Brightly colored markers are lined up with military precision. Good-luck charms—stuffed animals, framed pictures of grandchildren, aromatherapy candles in beaded holders—adorn each place. Many of the women have beside them bingo bags, drawstring satchels with holsters on the outside to hold their markers. These people look like they've been here all day, and to a certain extent, they have. One of the very helpful attendants explains that while the doors open at 9 A.M., people begin arriving and lining up as early as 7 A.M. As I survey the scene, it occurs to me I have overlooked one crucial element in all my bingo bravado: The competition is going to be fierce.

At the admissions window, I pay my fifty-five-dollar fee and, in turn, am handed a pad of fifteen newsprint bingo sheets, one bonus sheet, and a special bingo bonanza card. It takes some doing for the doorman to find me a space, but finally I am shown to a seat in the middle of a table in the middle of row after row of folding banquet tables. Clutching my sheaf of papers, I give him a quick, desperate look that implies, "You're not going to leave me here, are you?" But he is off, swallowed back into the swirl of milling people, and I'm on my own.

Now, I'm not always the most outgoing person, but I feel I have no choice but to quickly bond with my bingo mates or forever get lost in the dust. "Hi," I say, perhaps a little too loudly, to anyone in earshot of my seat. "I have absolutely no idea what I'm doing."

Luck is on my side. I have been seated next to Lori and Steve, a young engaged couple who won tickets to today's game in a raffle. Lori wears glasses, and has dark, dark hair and a sweet smile. A Penobscot raised on Indian Island, but now living in Houlton, she seems to either know or be related to most of the workers. She points to a woman selling feathers, little leather canoes, and beaded dolls in one of the many concessions stalls. "That's my cousin," she says, pleased, as she smiles and waves. I ask Lori why the players arrive so early. "To get a good seat," she suggests. And what do they do? She shrugs. "I don't know. Socialize. Eat." Her voice trails off.

Steve is a large man, with dark eyes and hair, and also has a quick and easy smile. Seated across from me is Frank, an older congenial gentleman from Plymouth (Maine, not Massachusetts, he stresses), who says he plays bingo, on average, twice per week. All three assure me I'll catch on.

I'm not so sure. I assess my bingo ephemera. For some reason, I thought I'd have one card in front of me, and all I'd have to do was fill in a straight line to win. Ho ho ho, Bingo Weenie, think again. Each of my newsprint sheets has twelve bingo cards printed on it, which means I will have to keep twelve games going at once. As for simple straight lines—forget about it. The lineup of games on the roster, the prizes for which range from $200 to two $25,000 jackpots, bear such names as "Champagne Glass," "Double Bingo Quinella," "Crazy T," "Picnic Table," "Coverall" and "Three Candles." Winning is no longer the issue. I'm just worried about how to play. A veneer of sweat suddenly covers my skin. I think my lower lip is trembling when I meekly inquire, "Champagne Glass?"

From my three new friends, I get a quick primer. Frank explains that each of these game names represents the pattern I'll have to make on a card. He points out a large scoreboard on the wall behind us, which will show the required pattern and also post the numbers that have been called. I notice a number of cash awards are for $1,199 and ask why. He explains those are called "beat the system" games, since there are no taxes on winnings under $1,200. I'm next enlightened on the subject of "specials" and "quickies," separately purchased games that take place between regular play. I don't feel I can handle this extra responsibility, but Steve points out that since I'm here, I might as well go for the whole shootin' match. All right then. I'm in. Frank flags one of the attendants roaming around the floor—mostly young women—and informs her I want to purchase some specials and quickies. There's a flurried exchange of paper and cash, and I add the new games to the ones piled in front of me. This bingo racket suddenly strikes me as a lot of work.

I'm ready now to play, but I must first wait out the end of the warm-up round. I go purchase a Dab-O-Ink marker, which resembles a liquid-shoe-polish applicator, from one of the novelty booths and then wander around. The hall is festooned with giant dreamcatchers, feathered hoops suspended from the ceiling. The air is thick with the smell of fried food and cigarette smoke. (There are non-smoking sections available, but in this open-air space, they, too, become stinky by the end of the day.) Signs around the outer wall advertise the sale of Pull Tabs, games that work like lottery scratch cards, except you rip open perforated tabs to reveal your prize. I purchase a handful and go through my stack in minutes for a net gain of fifty cents.

Those not participating in the warm-up are, indeed, socializing or eating. Boxes and bags and packages of snack food are spread over the tables. One player quietly reads a copy of the *Bingo Bugler* newspaper. A number of women solemnly knit and chat. One wears a pin that declares: "Bingo forever. Housework whenever."

These people mean business.

At last, regular play begins. The first game up is a special, the ominous "Champagne Glass." The figure comes up on the overhead board and I sketch it, in pencil, on my twelve games. When the first number is called, I notice my bingo mates have already filled it in. They then point out various small TV screens positioned around the hall that show the number before it's announced. Now I get it. Watch the screen. B-7. I scan my sheet and go at the numbers with my purple marker. It makes round splats the color of blueberry pie. Another number is called. And another. Each time I go into a stamping frenzy. Eventually I get the hang of it. Just as I'm starting to feel comfortable, I hear "BINGO!" called from across the room. There's a pause. One of the attendants goes to the table, checks the sheet, and radios back to the announcer that it's legitimate.

"That's a good bingo," the sonorous voice booms over the P.A.

"That is *not* a good bingo," I growl under my breath, as I rip the top sheet from my pad and crumple it into the plastic garbage bag by my side.

Another special is played, and another special is won (not by me). Next is a quickie, during which the announcer swiftly calls numbers, but no letters, and you must fill in all your squares. I am in a panic to keep up. My eye darts back and forth from the board to my card. Another good bingo is called. More crumpled paper. This puts me in somewhat of a huff, but there's not a sign of discouragement on any of the faces of the players around me. It's as though, for them, each game is a fresh start in which anything is possible.

As the games go on, I notice an almost melodic ebb and flow to the play. Between each game there is a thrum of noise—people shifting, chatting, kissing talismans, pulling up lucky socks, whatever helps them keep the positive energy flowing—but the instant a number appears on the screen, a dead hush falls across the room. As subsequent numbers are called, the air grows more and more charged. Then you detect a very low rumble: It's the sound of someone alerting her neighbors she's closing in on bingo. Then there's a cry, someone wins, and the process starts all over. Silence, tension, rumble, BINGO! It's hypnotic, numbing.

I must confess that after getting my bingo feet wet, I really enjoy my first few games. I, too, feel the sunny optimism of a new round of play, but as the afternoon wears on, as the break comes and goes, the novelty of the experience begins to wane, and I grow restless. My mind wanders. My neck is strained from hunching over my bingo sheets. I want to sit out a round, but what if the one I choose to miss is my one chance at a winner? No, I stay seated, relentlessly making purple dots, my eyes stinging from cigarette smoke, and my head aching from concentrating. Only once in my thirty-three rounds of play do I ever come near— within two squares—of winning, but before I can even alert my bingo pals, I once again hear the dreaded BINGO.

At last, the final jackpot of the day is called. It's going on 7 P.M., and many of these players will be returning tomorrow for the second half of their weekend, but my quest is over. After I inch my way off Indian Island in the long line of traffic and finally arrive at open highway, I clutch the wheel and let out a resounding BINGO! just to see how it feels.

In the end I guess it's best I didn't catch the bingo bug. I sound like an absolute weenie.

[2001]

Udder Nonsense

There are any number of things my grandfather—a farming man born in 1886—would not get about the world today: paying a dollar for a bottle of water, pedaling yourself to nowhere on a stationary bike, or feeling the need to yabber into a cell phone everywhere you go.

What might most confound him, however, is the notion that people would willingly lay down good cash money to go stay on someone else's farm and, worse, do their chores for them.

But that's exactly my desire. Even though my childhood included visits to my grandparents' farm in Gorham, by the time I came along, operations there had been scaled back to a few gentleman-farmer's rows of corn and beans. There were no chickens to torment, hay bales to dive into, tractors to ride on, and, most lacking, no cows to milk. I feel the time has come to make up for this deficiency in my catalog of Maine experiences.

Fortunately, a number of farmers (or farm owners) all over the state are opening their doors, barns, and pastures to visitors seeking a rural alternative to standard lodging options. Many of these are represented by the Maine Farm Vacation B&B Association, and, using their brochure as my guide, I am able to quickly narrow the field. While all guarantee a hearty breakfast and peace and quiet, not all, I note, are working farms. Some are simply inns in agrarian settings, with features such as full liquor licenses or saunas. Many of those that are working farms focus on specialty foods, garden produce, orchards, hay fields, llamas, or beef cattle. All this sounds very nice, but I want cows.

Then one listing catches my eye: "…an old-fashioned, small, one-family working farm… [that] includes milking cows that are milked by hand."

Milked by *hand*. I've found my spot.

When I telephone Flossie Howard at Ken-Rose Farm in Blue Hill, she tells me that if I want to milk a cow, I can either get up in the middle of the night for the 3 A.M. session or arrive by 2 P.M. for the afternoon one. Without pause, I tell her I'll see her around noon. I don't, after all, want to take this farmhand thing too far.

On the appointed day, I depart U.S. Route 1 outside of Orland for the Blue Hill Peninsula and enter into one of the many pockets of Maine farm country. Route 15 rises and falls, passing dense stands of trees and wide-open fields. Following my host's directions, I keep my eyes peeled for a white 1850s Cape, a big barn, and a small herd of Jerseys. Minutes later, there they are. I slow and crunch into the gravel drive.

Sasha and Lady, two aging and friendly dogs that make up just part of the Ken-Rose menagerie, come loping over to greet me. I go to the kitchen door, where I meet Flossie, a pleasant and cheery woman, who welcomes me like family. She moves slowly and stiffly as she guides me to the staircase and my room. "Uncle Arthur," she says over her shoulder, referring to the arthritis that plagues her. In fact, when we talk again later, she tells me that they're in the process of cutting back the B&B part of Ken-Rose Farm, and that the only reservations they'll be accepting are from repeat visitors or people with family in the area. "We're both getting old," she explains, "and I'd like to finally know what it's like to sit out on that back deck of ours, for a change."

But that doesn't seem to slow her down now. There's a list of chores to be tackled before day's end, and she'll be up at the crack of dawn to turn out batch after batch of her award-winning cinnamon rolls to be sold to an organic market in Blue Hill. She takes it all in stride and good humor. A sign hanging in the kitchen reads: "I can only please one person per day. Today is not your day. Tomorrow doesn't look good either."

I have arrived with sufficient time to look around and explore the grounds before the 2 P.M. milking. I stow my bag in my room, which is cozy enough to make even an urbanite feel like Rebecca of Sunnybrook Farm, and set out to snooping.

Ken-Rose Farm is sited on 150 acres, with an additional twenty acres of blueberry fields located down the road. Much of the acreage is cow pasture, fringed by woods and a small stand of aged apple trees. In back of the house, ducks splash in a plastic wading pool near a rabbit pen, which contains some orphaned bunnies the Howards have taken in. Between the barn and the pasture is a modest garden plot, all riotous with its height-of-summer growth, and a turkey pen containing forty-five geeky-necked, beady-eyed white birds. I walk over to the pen, and the turkeys make a mad dash to check me out, but by the time they arrive, they have forgotten what they came for. (Turkeys are not exactly the Einsteins of the animal kingdom.)

I work my way back to the house, and there I meet Kendall Howard, a slight man dressed in a faded plaid shirt and Dickies, who is accompanied by Flossie's teenage grandson, Dale, who spends his summers helping out on the farm. (Flossie and Kendall's marriage is the second for both of them; they've been married just over ten years.)

At seventy-three, Kendall is the youngest of twelve children and was born in the Ken-Rose living room. He says he has been milking cows since he was four years old. "Milking is the laziest job on the farm," he says with a wry smile. "It's the one you get to do sitting down."

We have a little time left before the prompt 2 P.M. milking, so Kendall escorts me around the barn, where hay is piled high to the rafters and Blue Seal feed bags are bundled and stacked. There are a couple cords of wood that have arrived earlier in the day, waiting to be stacked. The air is sweet, smelling a little of chamomile tea. Dust hangs suspended in the shafts of sunlight, and various tools and assorted tack are stored without total regard to order. Here, in this barn, time has stopped. We couldn't be farther away from exercise equipment and electronics. Blink, and it's fifty years past. Blink again, and it's a hundred.

Kendall brings me around to a pen to visit the chickens. We inspect the leghorns, the bantams, and the Rhode Island Reds. Having once been chased by a chicken (hence my poultry issues), I eye these birds suspiciously, but Kendall looks upon them as though they were cuddly kittens.

At last, it's milking time. Kendall, Dale, and I enter the stable, where the cows are lined up, their names displayed over each stall: Sibyl, Vicki, Cricket, Marilyn, Shenandoah, Darcy. Ribbons from county fairs are pinned here and there. The ceiling is low, and there is a newfangled fly strip that runs along its length. It looks like a retractable clothesline, except there's a hand crank on one end that reels in the gummy fly carcasses and presents a clean length of line with fresh goo at the other. At the far end of the stable, two stout pigs snort in a stall. A hefty can of Bag Balm sits on a window ledge that looks out on a large pile of manure—or "dressing," as Kendall calls it. The smell is heady.

As we get ready for the milking, Dale leaves us to go tackle the pile of wood. Although he helps with every other aspect of the farm, milking holds no interest for him. "Just doesn't appeal to me," he says with a shrug and departs.

Kendall sets to work. There is a clear procedure to this milking business. He first sprays the cows down with insecticide and then brushes them. As he goes about these second-nature chores, he talks cows to me. He says, on average, it takes him five or six minutes to fill a pail. He also tells me Jerseys are known for their high butterfat production (which could explain why people come from far and wide to purchase the Howards' famous homemade butter). Looking at all the ribbons on the walls, I ask him what makes a prize-winning cow.

Kendall casts an admiring glance at Vicki's backside. "A straight leg. A square bag," he says, running a hand over Vicki's udder. I hope he doesn't see me blush.

He next unhooks his milking stool from the wall and swings a galvanized pail under Vicki, who is, according to him, the leader. Using a warm cloth, he washes the udder before the milking. With that final task completed, he's ready.

"Step up girl," he gently urges, patting her and speaking with a kindly bedside manner. "Just one step." Almost without thinking, it seems, he cradles a teat and gives it a gentle tug. A sure, steady stream fires into the bucket, causing it to ring. He works on the one teat for a few pulls, and then his other hand drifts up to another, almost with the elegance of a concert pianist. Suddenly the streams are at a crossfire. The milk begins to fill the pail, and the ringing sound turns into a frothy *slursh*. Cow and man are lost in the ancient ritual. Vicki's tail occasionally swats him in the face, but he doesn't seem to notice. "People think milking's easy," he eventually says, giving me a smart smile. I observe his handiwork. There does not look like there's one thing easy about any of this.

Next, it's my turn. Kendall, with no small effort, removes himself from the milking stool and sets it down in front of another cow. We switch positions, awkward in that narrow space as passengers moving by one another on a crowded bus. I bump into the cow, Kendall eases out and I take my place. I have selected, as part of my inaugural milking outfit, my trusty Wellies (which I've dubbed my "milking slippers" for the day), but my cow, Sibyl, does not seem impressed.

I face the freckled teat. There is something kind of, well, icky about it, but I gingerly take it in my grasp and give it a gentle pull. Nothing. Sibyl continues to seem unimpressed and, happily, unperturbed. I give another tug, this time with a bit more oomph, as though I were ringing for the butler. A pathetic dribble hits the pail. Kendall moves behind me, takes me by the shoulders and says, "That's all right, honey." The "honey" part makes me feel like less of a failure. He repositions my fingers, and I give yet another tug, and then another. At last, a barely perceptible stream of milk trickles into the bucket. Before I know it, there is a good thimbleful in the bottom of my pail. But I have done it. I have officially milked a cow.

Not wanting to further delay Kendall's milking, I join Dale, who is stacking wood. I ask him if I can help, but he declines, simply saying, "No, that's what grandsons are for." I notice the sound of a radio in the background, and Dale explains it's kept on to keep the cows company. I don't want to, but have to ask what the cows' favorite station is. Dale strides right into my gaping straight line without pause. "Country Western," he says, with a toothy grin. "Of course."

After the milking is done, the girls are put back out to pasture, and Kendall dreamily watches them file off. "That's one of my favorite sights," he says, and it instantly becomes one of mine, as well.

When he's done with the wood, Dale offers to walk me up the road, so I can see the blueberry fields. As we stroll along Route 15, the cars whizzing by, he tells me he has no interest in leaving the area when he finishes high school. He pauses for a minute and then says, "It's quiet here. You're away from phones and computers." I want to wrap up this kid and ship him off to the Smithsonian.

But he has the point exactly right. Later, as I settle down into my bed for the night, I assess my day. So I didn't exactly take a blue ribbon for my milking efforts. And I didn't work up a sweat toiling in the fields. But I did find the promised quiet and calm, and I was given the opportunity to spend some time with genuinely nice people who understand and preserve the pleasures of living so close to the land.

And that's something even my grandfather would understand and admire.

[2001]

Toll Taker for a Day

I can't decide what to wear. Jeans and a polo shirt have been recommended, but I don't wear jeans and I haven't owned a polo shirt since the last time I picked up a golf club, sometime in the mid-1980s. A swingy skirt is out of the question. I fear an updraft from a passing tractor-trailer truck would send it sailing over my head. In the end, I select a pair of black trousers, black Converse high-tops, and a T-shirt. When I finish dressing, I inspect myself in the mirror. No, I don't much look like an official Maine Turnpike Authority (MTA) toll taker, but the outfit will have to do. I am expected at the Exit 9 toll plaza in Falmouth soon, and I don't want to be late for my big day.

Now, I've held many jobs over the years. My first was manning the tourist information booth on Route 1 outside Bath. I've worked in retail and restaurants. I've been a bellhop, a night watchman, and a landscaper's assistant. I even served a two-night stint working as a hat-check girl at the then Sonesta Hotel in Portland. But throughout all my occupational dabblings, the job of toll taker was one that had never made so much as a blip on my radar—that is, until recently, when a friend asked if I had ever noticed how pleasant Maine toll collectors are. I guessed I had, but it was something I'd never given much thought. The question sparked my curiosity.

What, I wondered, was life like in those glass booths? Who were these people? Why *were* they so pleasant? How did they get their jobs? Was the pay good? Did the noise and exhaust fumes bother them? Did they get bored? What did they do if they forgot their lunch? How did they deal with irate motorists? What about the endless cootie contact of hands and money? More than anything, however, I wanted to know what they did when they had a line of cars backed up and they had to use the bathroom.

And, now, as I approach the exit, I am about to find out. Firsthand.

I arrive at 11 A.M. on an overcast July morning. I'm waved past the toll window to the parking area (yes, I feel like a big shot) and am met by Gary Frederick, who will oversee my shift, and who is the supervisor at Exit 9, otherwise known as the "coastal connector" to Route 1 from the turnpike. Frederick, 57, is a wiry and outgoing man with a quick, bright smile. He is wearing, yes, jeans and a polo shirt, as well as sneakers and wire-framed glasses. A Maine Turnpike Authority cap is perched upon his head, and a blaze-orange mesh vest completes his uniform.

Before we begin, he asks if I wouldn't mind waiting a couple of minutes in the staff break room—a small trailer located adjacent to the brick building that houses the plaza office and bathroom—while he makes the rounds to see if the two other toll takers working that day require a break. (There's one question answered.)

It's close in the trailer, and the mini-blinds are lowered. It has the usual trappings: chairs and a table, a TV (with rabbit ears), a toaster oven, microwave, refrigerator, and water cooler. Next to the coffee maker, a sign posted on a tin can reads: "Coffee, 25 cents. Cash Only." I peer in and count four quarters.

As I wait, I watch Frederick from the window as he deftly handles the stream of cars and trucks that pass through his booth. There is an economy to his every movement, and that smile never leaves his face. Here's a man, I think, who loves his job.

And, according to MTA Public Affairs Director Dan Paradee,

Frederick is not alone. The Maine Turnpike Authority employs 297 toll takers at its sixteen toll plazas. Of those workers, 173 are full time (some with as many as fifteen or twenty years of service behind them); 96 are part time/on-call; and 26 are I.P.s (Intermittent Part-timers: toll collectors who are assured a forty-hour work week, but move around from plaza to plaza as needed). There's about a fifty-fifty split between male and female personnel. The starting pay is $11 per hour and tops out at $14 per hour, with full health benefits, including dental. New hires start out as I.P.s and are given one week of on-the-job training. Seniority usually dictates who gets the permanent gigs and who is promoted to supervisor. Anyone with a high school diploma (or GED) who is at least eighteen years of age may apply. Prior work experience helps, but is not required. What the MTA really looks for is reliability, friendliness, the ability to work independently, and the capacity to care for the safety and convenience of MTA customers—fitting attributes for Maine's unofficial Ambassadors of Transit.

When Frederick comes to collect me, I am given my own blaze-orange vest and am instructed on proper toll-crossing techniques. We stand at the head of the crosswalk as a passenger car finishes its transaction and moves on. A semi slowly rumbles up, yet we do not move. "You have to make eye contact," Frederick says, looking up into the cab and getting the high sign from the driver. We then scoot across to the concrete island on which our booth is sited, take a look down the lane to ensure no cars are coming, and enter.

The booth's interior mildly resembles a steering cabin on a boat, but at each end there's a counter, a money drawer, and a touch-screen computer. Handwritten mileage charts, exit numbers, and Canadian exchange rates are posted on the wall. A swivel stool is pushed in the corner. It doesn't look like it gets much use.

Frederick first gives me the lay of the land. He logs his employee number onto the screen, slides his drawer (he's been on the job this day since 5 A.M.) into the till and announces we're open for business. The screen operation is also straight-forward. As a vehicle approaches, you assess its class, which is determined by its number of axles and if it has anything in tow. Passenger cars, vans, and motorcycles, for example, are Class 1. A truck with a two-wheeled camper in tow is Class 7. Toll collectors, it seems, do a lot of tire counting.

Once you have assessed the vehicle's class, you enter it onto the screen, and the appropriate fare pops up. You collect the toll, touch the "fare paid" command, and start the process all over again. Frederick explains all this as he keeps the flow of traffic moving. A Class 2 truck approaches. By the time the driver has his money out, Frederick has a receipt ready and waiting. "If you see advertising on a vehicle," he says, "you know they'll want a receipt." As I stand behind him, watching over his shoulder, he tests me on classes. A semi approaches. I count five sets of tires and, feeling not just a little pleased with my toll-taking precocity, chirp, "Class 5!" Frederick enters a Class 4 onto the screen. "Look again," he says, gesturing to the back set of tires, which are jacked up. "The tires have to be touching the road to count," he says.

After a while, however, I start to get it. When there's a break in the traffic, Frederick decides it's time for me to man the helm. I assume my post—feet shoulder-width apart, hands poised over the drawer like a keyboard. Bring on the cars!

A vehicle approaches, a sedan. I touch the "Class 1" command, lean out, collect the fifty cents with a perhaps-too-robust "Thank you!" and press "paid." I'm disappointed I don't get to test my change-making abilities, but that will come. Frederick explains a lot of people prefer to come to the manned booths, rather than throwing the money in the basket of the automated ones. He shrugs. "Don't ask me why."

Soon, things pick up. Change is made—and not just quarters. Each class represents a different fare, often involving wily dimes and nickels. Directions are asked. (The most common at this exit: "How far to/what exit is L.L. Bean?") Wheels are counted. Every so often I get stumped on class, such as when a pick-up with dual rear tires approaches. I give Frederick a helpless look. Those dual tires make it a Class 2, I am told, and I feel a little chagrined I didn't figure that out on my own. A car whooshes by without so much as slowing. "Hey!" I call after it (as though my girly "Hey!" would cause a driver to stop). Frederick taps me on the shoulder and points to the word "Transpass" on the screen. "Transpass vehicles can use any lane," he says. If humans blushed orange, my face would've matched my vest.

After about fifteen minutes, I am given a break. I step aside and cast a glance down at my hands, which are trembling—no, shaking. Frederick finishes with our line of cars, and then we move on to another booth to spell one of the other toll takers for his lunch break. Cash drawers are switched with pit-stop speed and precision; the line of waiting cars moves without interruption.

I ask Frederick, who has worked for the MTA since 1994, why he became a toll taker. He says he had been the manager for a chain of variety stores in the Westbrook area for fourteen years and was ready for a change. His wife was the one who suggested the job. He applied and was hired. It took Frederick only a short time to work his way up the ranks. Three years in, the supervisor's job at Exit 9 came up, he threw his hat into the ring and was awarded the position. He says it was like a dream come true.

And to watch him work, it's clear he means it. A woman rolls up in her SUV and, offering a straight line as wide as the County, asks if this road will take her to Rockland. "Yes it will," he responds and adds, "You may want to turn every once in a while." An older man hands Frederick a dollar and announces he'd like a dollar-fifty in change. Frederick laughs and says, "Nice work if you can get it." A trucker leans down, hands him a fifty, and apologizes. "Not a problem!" Frederick says.

He does admit he occasionally has to deal with irate motorists—people irked about having to "pay to wait" or about the price of the tolls—but he does his best to try to lighten the situation. If he encounters motorists who can't be appeased, he'll direct them to a higher-up in the MTA and give them a number to call. Mostly, he says, these run-ins are infrequent, adding, "If you're nice to people, they're nice to you."

The traffic has slowed some—a rare occurrence in high summer, according to my boss—and I drill him with more questions. What happens when people don't have the fare? They fill out a "no funds" form and are asked to mail in their toll—on the honor system. What about germs? Frederick says he applies a simple tenet: You keep your hands away from your face, and you wash up during your breaks. (I also notice bottles of hand sanitizer in a number of the booths.) Boredom? He admits it can be a problem for some—particularly on the late-night shifts. (Toll takers are not supposed to watch TV or read on the clock.) I ask what he considers the greatest challenge of the job. He thinks a moment and says he imagines for most of the workers it's being on their feet for eight hours. He pauses. "But not for me. I've been working on my feet all my life."

I throw out one of my personal pet peeves: people who engage toll takers in conversation when there's a back-up. Frederick says he uses common sense. If people need to know an exit or quick directions, he'll supply them. If they want more detailed information, he'll apologize and point them to an exit where they can get help. (He stresses toll takers are prohibited from recommending specific lodging, dining, or other business establishments.) He says it takes only a moment to assist these motorists, and he can usually move them through in as much time as it takes to make change, which makes me a bit ashamed of my peeve.

I can't imagine everyone has the right toll-taker stuff like Frederick, but as I man my booth, I discover a couple of surprising things: First, I'm pretty good at this job. My wheeling and dealing change and receipts makes me feel like a Las Vegas blackjack dealer. Second, without exception, every person I encounter during my shift is at least mildly pleasant. Almost everyone gives a hello or thank-you. In fact, the most annoying encounter I have in my three hours is with a young woman who is yakking on a cell-phone headset when she pulls up to the window and takes a minute before she even notices me. Finally, she glances up with a blank look. "Fifty cents, please," I say, and she starts rummaging around for her wallet. As she hands me a dollar, she says, "I didn't realize I was at a toll booth."

The time flies by. Confident in my abilities, Frederick even leaves me on my own for a time, while he deals with a printer crisis in another booth. When he returns, he announces I have saved the day. "I'm not sure what we would've done if we didn't have your booth open. Traffic would've been backed up." I think he may be laying it on a bit thick, but my little toll-taking heart still swells with pride.

Finally, it's nearing the end of Frederick's shift, and my time with him is almost done. I'm not saying he has to exactly pry me from my post, but I am reluctant to go. When he escorts me back to the parking lot (we both now make eye contact with motorists as we cross), I retire my vest, and we shake hands. As we do, I lean in and say, "You guys ever get stuck, you give me a call. I'm right down the road. I could be here in minutes." He laughs and says he will.

And as the Exit 9 toll plaza fades in my rear-view mirror, I smirk and think: Won't *this* look good on my résumé?

[2002]

The Ultimate Moose Safari

The first of my two alarms sounds sharply at 4 A.M. I switch it off, grope for the light beside my bed, and, with closed eyes, flick it on. I have seven minutes before the next alarm goes off. I do not move, savoring these final, fleeting moments of repose. Finally, just before the second alarm, I roll myself out of bed and onto the floor (an old trick from my long-ago college days, when rising for a 10 A.M. class was often a challenge). I have no time to dawdle. I am expected at the Maine Guide Fly Shop, just down the road from my motel in Greenville, in a matter of minutes. I am about to embark on my first-ever, official moose safari.

Moose watching is big business in the Moosehead Lake area. The region's brochures shout out offers to get you up close and personal to these gawky kings and queens of Maine's North Woods. You can view moose by plane. You can paddle to them in a kayak or canoe. You can observe them from the comfort of a pontoon party boat (replete with refreshments and a head). You can use the map in the Moosehead visitor's guide, with its demarcated primo moose-sighting spots, and set out on your own. You could probably even slip the guy who pumps your gas a couple of bills, and he'd take you out to see a moose.

But none of these methods awaits me on this day. I am going moose watching with a Registered Maine Guide who has added his own unique twist to these excursions; I am going to float to my moose.

I pad across the motel room's carpeted floor to the gear I laid out last night: purple polypropylene long underwear, wool socks, fleece vest, hiking boots. I begin to dress, adding to the mix a T-shirt and a short yellow skirt. Okay, so I look like a clown, but this is no time for fashion worries. A quick brush of the teeth, and I'm off.

I shakily pull my car out of the motel entrance onto Route 6 for the two-minute drive down to town and the fly shop. I would describe the beauty of Moosehead Lake, with its scattering of small, sprucy islands, as viewed from Indian Hill at 4:25 A.M., but the sky is only starting to soften from its dark blue into a deep violet, and I can't see anything beyond the cut of my headlights. It is *very* early.

I enter the lot and am directed into a parking space by Dan Legere, my guide for the moose watch. The other members of the party—Brent, a large and strapping friend of Legere's, and photographer Richard Procopio—are already assembled and waiting. Legere, 50, is a trim and sturdy man with wire-frame glasses and a silver mustache. He at once strikes me as capable and in control, particularly when he takes one look at me as I stumble out of my car and guides me across the street to a gas station for coffee. The store, he informs me, opens at 3 A.M. for the early-rising loggers and fishermen in the area. And he should know. A well-respected fishing guide, Legere is often up at this hour and says he can't ever sleep much beyond 5:00 or 5:30.

When we return to the trucks, gear is stowed, and we prepare to head out. I will ride with Legere, it is decided, and I climb up onto the bench seat of his big beige Ford truck. This is a man's truck, a vehicle owned by someone accustomed to bumping down dirt roads. I lean back, trying not to slop my coffee, and wait for the show to begin.

There had been some joking in the parking lot about the potential dangers of this mission. At the time, it seemed nothing more than a bit of "scare the girl" (I have two older brothers and am used to this sort of ribbing), but now it occurs to me that I have absolutely no idea what

I'm in for. I don't know where we're headed. I don't know how close we'll be getting to the moose. I'm not even entirely sure how we'll be getting to them. All I've been told is that we're going to wear waders and use floats. I turn to Legere and say, "I don't know what I'm getting myself into here." He stares out the windshield, smiles quickly, and says, "It's better left that way."

Of course, he's only kidding. He assures me there's absolutely no threat of danger—except if we get between a cow and her calf: a mishap, he says, that will not happen on his watch. But I worry for a minute. What if I do something stupid and put myself there. Legere takes this opportunity to tell me a bit about moose. First of all, he says, moose have no predators—aside from man—in this region. Thus, they have two forms of defense: charge or stand their ground. A moose, he says, will give you good warning if you've ruffled him. There's a lot of posturing that goes on—stamping, scratching the ground—before a moose will charge. (Interpretation: If you don't heed the warnings, you might just deserve to get stomped on.)

Just then, Legere hits the brakes and wheels his head around. "A bull," he says. "Back there. Did you see it?" I did not. He is tempted for a minute to back up, but the morning is already starting to move on us, and we don't want to miss our moose-watching window. Moose, he informs me, are nocturnal. He says the two best times to see them are early morning and early evening. He himself prefers the morning. It's less crowded. It's more of an event, an adventure. Besides, some moose don't even get up until dark. We will be catching them at the end of the feeding, before they head back to the woods to snooze and get out of the heat. By nine o'clock, most of them will have retreated. But our timing is right, Legere says, and the conditions are perfect. There's a low-lying fog lingering that will help camouflage us and mask our scent. (I wonder if he knows I didn't take the time to shower this morning.)

We arrive at Legere's secret putting-in place, a friend's camp off a dirt road somewhere between Greenville and Kokadjo. Legere asks that I not reveal the directions to his moose-watching spot to save it from

being spoiled by too many visitors. He needn't worry. With my groggi-
ness and the darkness, I have no more idea where I am than if I had
been blindfolded.

It is still pre-dawn, but the sky is lightening and is tinged with pink.
We start hauling gear down to the shore, and this is when I first get to
assess what awaits. Three giant inner tubes with seats in them—or pontoon floats—will be our mode of transport for the actual watch. To
get us there, a small motorboat is dragged down to the water. Brent
affixes the motor. The bulk of the gear is loaded into a canoe, which
we will tow. There are many trips from truck to shore. This is no small
operation.

We climb aboard and head out into the dense fog, just as the sun
starts to poke up over the horizon like an orange thumbnail. The mist
hovers in long rolls at the foot of the black silhouetted hills that encir-
cle us. Legere makes a straight passage, unfazed that we can't see five
feet in front of us. We are headed for what he calls a "hole" that will
take us to his secret spot, which makes me feel like we are en route to
never-never land. Normally, I am not comfortable being transported in
a vehicle when I can't see where we're going, but something tells me
Legere could make this trek with his eyes closed.

Suddenly, he slows and cuts the motor. To our left, perched on the
top limb of a dead tree, shrouded in fog, is a bald eagle. I train my
binoculars on him. In the thick soup, it's hard to make out the bird's features, aside from the fact he is large, until a shaft of orange sun breaks
through the mire and illuminates his white crown. Then slowly, almost
lethargically, he takes wing and is gone. "Yep, just on cue," says Legere.
"Remind me to pay the bird trainer on the return trip."

Finally, we arrive at our destination. We are instructed to move as
quickly and quietly as we can. Legere has already spotted the outlines
of a couple of moose on the opposite shore, and we still have substan-
tial preparations before we can head out.

I suppose anyone who has fly-fished would be familiar with the
drill that is about to follow. Legere has adapted fly-fishing pontoon

floats for moose watching. First, I am handed a pair of spongy, insulated waders and a pair of fishing boots, which resemble standard work boots, but with felt covering the soles. I hop in the tall grass from rock to rock, until I find one large and flat enough to secure my footing. I remove my own boots and start working my way into the thick, snug waders, which look like big puffy footy pajamas. One foot and leg go in without a problem. As I try to tug on the second, however, my long johns ride up to my knee. Balanced precariously on my rock, with my arm shoved down inside the waders trying to tuck the leg of my underwear into the top of my sock is no easy business. Finally, success. I stand upright, pull up the bib, and buckle it. I finish off the outfit with the boots and my pith helmet (this is a safari, after all, isn't it?) and then look over to the next rock, where Procopio has apparently been watching. He pauses a minute, then in a complete deadpan says, "Never done this before, have you?"

Legere calls in a soft voice, "Ready?" which I take to mean to follow him out into the mucky water. My boots are a little large, the waders are stiff, and the pond floor is gummy. I approach my float with all the grace of a Bog Thing.

I take a seat and water rushes into my lap. Legere takes my booted feet and straps fins to them. "That's your motor," he says. He next erects a frame of plastic tubing into a box shape around me. And, for the final touch, a camouflage cloth with air slits is draped over me. I feel like a piece of summer furniture that's about to be put away for the season.

Brent and Legere get settled into their gear, and Legere floats over to me and points in the general direction we'll be heading. He turns me around backwards and tells me to kick like a frogman. "Quiet little kicks," he adds. "Try not to break the surface of the water."

I do as I'm instructed, or so I think. We are still near to shore, and I keep hitting rocks and bottom. My fins break the surface of the water. I am getting nowhere. And not fast. Apparently there has been a conference, because Brent and Legere come back, and each take a side of my pontoon and start towing me, while Procopio follows in the canoe.

I am, at first, mildly offended by the men's help. I've been swimming since I was a tadpole, and I've still got a few good kicks left in me. But their tow gives me a chance to practice using my boot-footed fins and get accustomed to life under my camo tent. No offense to Legere and his contraptions, but if I were a moose and saw these three camo-blobs floating toward me, I'd keel over laughing.

But our buoyant blinds do the trick. We make our way across the pond, until Legere alerts us that we've come to our first viewing spot. Slowly I kick myself around and, for the first time, see our moose. The haze has not yet lifted, so they are still a bit hard to focus in on, but I can see the shape of two large cows feeding on the sodium-rich water grasses (their favorite treat) just below the surface. At this distance, they pay no attention to us. The great heads dip down into the water, nose around, and then resurface, with water cascading from their mouths. Legere decides we can move in closer. I am becoming better at kicking and move right along with the rest of our party. Now the moose have either scented or spotted us, because every so often one will fix her gaze in our direction, but it appears we have done little to disrupt their feeding.

Moose-watching is a fairly new phenomenon, according to Legere, who has been in Greenville for twenty years. He remembers when spotting a moose was an event. Clear-cutting, however, did a lot to boost the moose population, he says. Now not seeing a moose is nigh impossible, if you put yourself in the right place at the right time. He says he mounted a counter in his a truck a couple of years ago, because people would ask him how many moose he saw in a season. He figured that one year he saw roughly between 350 and 500. Legere also differentiates between "real" moose (those in their natural habitat) and "ditch" or "road" moose, those that have spent so much time being gawked at they are unimpressed with humans.

Moose also have a fairly predictable timetable. When spring arrives, they will begin feeding on the new vegetation along the roadside and slurping up the residual road salt. This is when you're most likely to see a moose from your car, he says, but it's also the time when most of the moose-car collisions occur. As spring turns to summer, those roadside plants get tougher and dusty from the traffic, and the moose seek out nice, tasty bogs for their meals. Then, as fall approaches—and with it, the cooling of the water—the plants in the bog will start to die off (a bog is just like a meadow, he says), and the moose will perform what Legere terms their "vanishing act." Almost like clockwork, come September 1, the moose will be gone for two weeks—perhaps gussying up for the rut (or mating season). Then, during the rut, the males will "set up shop": securing an area—roughing it up, trashing trees with their antlers, and marking the area with their powerfully scented urine. ("A big stench," according to Legere.) If no female takers show up, the bull will put his powerful snoot to work and will—like an ungainly Pepe Le Pew—follow the scent of the female, regardless of the path. This, explains Legere, is when you will most often find moose out of their habitat — walking down main streets in towns or showing up on football fields. It's also when a moose call works best, providing it's given by someone who knows how to talk to moose. Which Legere does.

He now demonstrates. The noise that comes out of him sounds like a cross between a honk and a hoot. But the call works. On cue, the cows raise their heads, take a look across the pond, and then resume their feeding.

As we are engaged with our moose, another moose-watch party paddles up in canoes. The guide from that group informs us there's a cow and her calf down on the next shoreline, but Legere decides it's too far to kick in our gear. (I fear this may be because of me. If this were a survivor show, I'm sure I'd be first to be voted off.) The men compare notes on our spot. Legere's record number of moose-sightings here is twenty-something, the other guide's is thirty-one. Sure, double-digits would've been nice today, but I'm perfectly happy with our two.

We finally doff our camo. The fog has completely burnt off, and the sun is climbing. Our photographer paddles in to get a closer shot at the moose. "Go straight at her," Legere instructs. "It's harder for them to detect your movement." Procopio takes slow, sure strokes with his paddle and freezes when one of the cows lifts her head. When he gets close enough, he starts photographing, until one moose slowly lumbers off, followed, not too long after, by the other.

Soon, our party is out-and-out lazing. An osprey hovers overhead and dives for his breakfast. A loon joins the fold and cautiously circles us. And then, on the shore, a flash of auburn red. It's a young male deer, who prances along the path. I remember an earlier moose remark Legere made: "Moose have nowhere to go and all day to do it." Now that I've completed my mission, I feel remarkably akin to the beasts.

The show is winding down. Casually we kick our way back to the boat and get ready to head out, although I'm not anxious to wrap this up. I take a couple more frog kicks, lean back, and think about the early rising, the sloshing coffee, the dark and bumpy truck ride, the heavy fog, the orange sun rising, the easy banter, the weird gear, and the crazy kicking. What better way, I wonder, could there be to seize a piece of Maine summer than hanging out in the North Woods with these good men on this fine day?

The moose sightings, as it turned out, were just a bonus.

[2002]

Getting Down and Dirty

Viewed from a distance, the scene looks not unlike the setting for a family reunion. Large white tents cover much of the grassy state-owned spit of land jutting out into dazzling Atkins Bay at the mouth of the Kennebec River, ten miles south of the small shipbuilding city of Bath. Tables and coolers are positioned around the grounds. A white flag bearing a red cross (a family crest?) hangs limply in the still August air. The members of the group—ranging from elders to schoolchildren—lounge in lawn chairs, sprawl on the grass, or quietly mill about. Classical music drifts from a tinny boom box, as sandwiches are passed around. Yup, this could be anyone's gathering.

Venture a little closer, however, and you might notice the pink plastic flamingo protruding from the crook of a shady maple. Or all the dustpans, buckets, paintbrushes, root clippers, scoops, trowels, and clipboards scattered about. Or that the flag bears the Cross of Saint George, and the music is from the seventeenth century. Or that this lunching group is congregated around a series of shallow, rectangular holes—an entire geometric patchwork of them—as though this were a multi-generational gravediggers' convention. Despite the fact there is an apparent shared kinship here and a whole lot of digging going on, it is neither of the aforementioned functions. This is a gathering of a different stripe.

What you would've stumbled upon is the archeological dig at Fort St. George, the principal settlement of the short lived (1607–'08) Popham Colony, and its team of dig devotees, which is made up of a mix of professional archeologists, students, local volunteers, and paying participants in the Maine State Museum Field School Program, who come from all over the country and around the corner and consider this work a holiday.

Now, it takes a particular type of person to want to spend his or her one or two weeks of precious summer vacation in, astride, or beside a dirt hole, especially when that time involves, not lounging, but digging, sweating, scraping, toiling, and toting—and paying for the privilege to do so. (The tuition for the field school program is $600 per week, which includes accommodations at a nearby B&B and meals, the preparation and clean-up of which are shared by all participants.)

Yet the field school attracts just that type of person each year for the coveted fifteen slots allotted for each of two weeks during the three-week dig. Many of these students are repeats; most of them sign on for both weeks. Those who can't invariably wish they could. This dig, it seems, is a vacation destination of choice for those of a particular ilk.

Of course, it would be hard to deny some of the appeal is the setting. Just around the bend from the dig, the snug summer colony at Popham Beach—with its dense thickets of beach roses, clustered cottages, general store, wee library, and spired church—is all Maine idyll. Sunbathers sprawl across the three miles of pristine sand beach, where low dunes bristle with spiky grass and the surf languorously rolls in. Down near Fort Popham—a granite fortress built during the Civil War—and Spinney's restaurant, the usual mix of fisherfolk are stationed at the water's edge. Some plant their rods in the sand and snooze under umbrellas. Others stand sentry, scanning the ocean's surface for signs of striper and bluefish. Toddlers splash and scream. Little do these vacationers (and most Mainers) know, however, is that just up the road an event of national historic significance is taking place. And, for those participating in the dig, that is the real appeal.

The project, which is sponsored in part by the Maine Historic Preservation Commission, is conducted under the capable leadership of Dr. Jeffrey Brain, a Ph.D. in archeology and anthropology and senior research associate at the Peabody Essex Museum in Salem, Massachusetts. Brain first "discovered" the largely forgotten Fort St. George site while vacationing in the area in the early 1990s. After an initial excavation in 1994, he felt he was on to something. He secured funding and started his dig in earnest in 1997. It has been going on every summer since.

Brain cuts an imposing figure. A large, wry man in faded, salmon-colored trousers, an oxford-cloth shirt, bright-red suspenders, and floppy hat, he patrols the site clutching a red-and-white striped stick, which he refers to as his "crew beater." When asked, he says he doesn't have to use the stick too often, with a deadpan that bespeaks his in-the-trenches humor. (He also has a sign posted on the fence surrounding the area: "Please do not feed the archeologists or rattle their cages.") It would seem these digs are not entirely dry, dusty affairs.

But they are labor-intensive and often rely heavily on lay help to get the job done, such as the field-school students and volunteers, who are—to put it plainly—the grunts. They are the ones down in the pits, doing the digging, the hauling of buckets of earth to the large sifter, the sifting itself, and the recording of data, which is later reviewed by one of the dig's professional assistants. Brain has worked with all sorts of teams, even convicts. "Never had a crew that complained so little," he says, almost wistfully, gazing into the distance. "But then, they couldn't say much, now could they?"

The Fort St. George site has special historic significance on a number of levels. First of all, it is the oldest English fort in the Northeast. It was settled by a party of aristocrats led by George Popham and Raleigh Gilbert in August 1607—the same year as Jamestown, Virginia. Jamestown, as every schoolchild knows, succeeded; the Popham Colony did not and became not much more than a historical footnote. A number of reasons have been attributed to the failure—food shortages, infighting, the death of Popham, the hellacious Maine winter, and Gilbert's departure to claim a family inheritance in the fall of 1608—but it is just this failure that makes it of archeological interest. Jamestown has been continually settled and, thus, its contents have been disturbed. Fort St. George, by comparison, has remained largely undisturbed, even though it was also the site of Fort Baldwin, a World War I military base. Consequently, it has been preserved as a time capsule of one of the major cornerstones of English-American history.

The most exciting aspect, however, is something unique to early English-American settlements: a map. Drawn on site by one of the settlers, John Hunt, this plan shows the positions of eighteen buildings with descriptions and, perhaps most important, a scale. The map was sent back to England in October of 1607, where the Spanish ambassador got his hands on a copy. He sent it to Spain, and it was thrown into the archives and forgotten. This rare, detailed document resurfaced in 1888, was published in 1890, and has served as an invaluable guide for the dig. It is not known how many of the structures were actually built. Brain's prior digs have confirmed the location of the colony's storehouse and the Gilbert house, but more remain to be discovered. And that's Brain's challenge.

Of course, none of this is news to anyone taking part. Most of the people here have been on digs before and share a love of archeology, learning, and history. They are also dedicated to Brain and this particular dig. But one just has to ask: Is it any fun?

"It's hard work," says Tim Dinsmore, a historical archeologist based in Damariscotta and one of Brain's professional assistants. "It's painstaking and meticulous. But the thing that motivates people is the knowledge each individual is contributing to a piece of history."

That may sound sort of corny, but he's right. Where some might find this type of vacation dull and dirty, these people look rapt. If you need evidence, get down on your hands and knees and belly up to one of the workers gently scraping her trowel toward her and ask if she's enjoying herself. Mary Concannon, for example, who is examining a "greasy" spot on the floor of her pit. A professional archeologist with short curly black hair and wearing grubby sneakers, Concannon is back for her fourth year. She likens what she's doing to reading a mystery, explaining the greasy spot could mean she has uncovered a hearth, but she's not going to go out on a limb quite yet, not until more clues are revealed. "It's sometimes not the guy you think it is," she says, perhaps as much to her greasy spot as to anyone. She's not being impolite; she's just clearly anxious to get back to her "book."

Many of the people here use one sort of book analogy or another to describe the dig. And because the pages of that book are held in the earth's strata, being able to read dirt is essential. The untrained eye might look into one of the pits and see nothing but uniform brown, but gaze deeper and you see the layers take on different qualities, as though various chocolate tortes and cakes were piled up and compressed on top of each other. In one layer, the earth is dark and dense; in another it's more the color of milk chocolate; in another it looks like coffee grounds. To the trained eye, these varying soils speak volumes.

One couple who has done their share of reading dirt is John Sturgis and his wife, Barbara, retirees from Arizona and students in the field school. They've traveled all over the country, very often combining family visits with their digs, according to John, who is enjoying the last few minutes of his lunch break in the chair he has brought along. "But the chair is crucial," he says. "It's not the getting dirty, which you do. It's the getting up and down."

But the appeal is not just for those schooled or experienced in archeology or those with extra leisure time on their hands. Just ask Merry Chapin, a teacher at the nearby Phippsburg Elementary School, who brings small groups of her fifth-grade class to observe and participate during the two weeks the dig is open. While the kids may not at first appreciate having a school function cut into the last days of their vacation, they quickly become enthralled. Chapin says both the volunteers and leaders are extremely generous with their knowledge and time and are more than willing to share it with these children. Soon the kids become deeply involved in the historical drama being played out in their backyard.

Same for Carrie Swan of Yarmouth, a student of classical archeology and anthropology at Dartmouth College, who is using her summer to get her dig feet wet. Freckled, her hair pulled back into a ponytail and sporting the same "I can't believe I get to be a part of this" look in her eye as the other participants, Swan feels like this is a dream come true. "I always played 'archeologist' when I was a kid," she says, smiling. "My father is a dentist, and he would bring home picks and tools for me to use." That early fascination has blossomed. Earlier in the summer, Swan had the opportunity to travel to Italy and dig at Pompeii, where she had the amazing good luck of finding an intact container. From that point on, she says, she was dubbed "Golden Trowel."

The artifacts turned up at Fort St. George—shards of pottery, stoneware, bottle glass, buttons, tiny clay pipes, pieces of lead, musket balls—may not be as glamorous as intact vessels, but they, along with the discovery of "features"—floors, walls, pits, postholes—are just as important. "It's not artifacts we're out for," says Brain, "it's information. What we are looking for is how people lived and what happened here." Of course, there are always going to be questions left unanswered, he says. But then, with archeology, it seems there's always a new set of questions with each turn of the trowel.

It's just those questions that will keep Brain and his "family" of dig devotees coming back. He plans to continue the project for a few more summers, and then he will concentrate on collecting and publishing his findings. Until then, however, he can count on a ready team at his side. And, judging by the looks in their eyes, he can quite safely leave his crew beater at home.

[2002]

Rubbing It In

There are any number of reasons why I wouldn't have considered myself the ideal candidate for a session at a day spa, not the least of which being I'm a Yankee. Hale Maine girls just don't give themselves over to a day or two of pampering, especially when said pampering entails paying good cash money for having one's nether-, hinter-, and thither-regions handled by strangers. No, such an indulgence, I thought, was not for me.

That is, until I had the opportunity to visit the brand-new Cliff House Resort & Spa, located on Maine's southern coast in Ogunquit. One of the state's oldest seaside resorts, The Cliff House, which is sited on seventy acres at Bald Head Cliff, started life in 1872 as one of those sprawling, multi-storied Victorian hotels and has been in the same family ever since. (Historic photos and mementos from the era feature prominently in the hotel's décor, giving you an idea of that more genteel time.) Over its long history, The Cliff House has seen numerous incarnations—the original hotel is no longer; today the compound is made up of an odd assortment of buildings and annexes, including boxy, barracks-like structures and a section that looks like a motel—but none, perhaps, as dramatic as this most recent one. Billing itself as "New England's first oceanfront spa," the Cliff House spa opened in

May of 2002, offering such enticements as indoor and outdoor swimming pools and whirlpools, steam rooms, saunas, a fitness center, rooms for massage, nail and skin care, and signature treatments inspired by Maine flora and the sea—all contained in a state-of-the-art facility with uninterrupted views of the Atlantic.

Yankee or not, I thought, sign me up.

I will tell you right now the planning of my retreat became a minor preoccupation. The number of options was dizzying. And there was the issue of time. Most treatments last about an hour. How many per day would be right? How much of a lull should I allow in between? Should I schedule a meal? Would there be time to do nothing? Important considerations all.

It took me a good week to nail down my selections, deciding, in the end, to sample one treatment from each category. (Look, if you're going to fall off the austerity wagon, you might as well go headfirst.) After a number of phone calls to the spa's reception desk, I finally opted for the following, based on their Maine-sounding attributes: for day one, the Cliff House Signature Facial, with blueberry smoothie mask; the Cliff House Hot Stone Massage, with seaweed oil and local stones from Bald Head Cliff; and the Juniper Berry Body Wrap—popular with both men and women. For day two, I chose the spa's signature manicure and pedicure, with their "special treatment" using seaweed paste. Most intriguing was an item called the "royal throne," which is used for the pedicure. My curiosity was officially piqued.

I arrive at the Cliff House at 9:30 on the appointed morning. The summer traffic in the tourist hub of Ogunquit is already thick, but I manage to creep my way through town and out around the torturously twisting hairpin turns on Shore Road. I follow the long, shaded drive to the resort's reception area and inform the desk I am on site, in the event I might be able to check in earlier than the guaranteed 3 P.M. My room— one of thirty-two new spa rooms, with king-size bed, gas-fired woodstove, and private deck—is not ready, but I am told to feel free to keep checking back. And I don't really need my own room to partake of all the spa treatments for which I've signed up. That's only for sleeping—in luxury I presume. I return to the parking area and look for the spa building.

I find my way over to the entrance, pass through a foyer to the tiled floor and polished wood of the spa's lobby. The light is soft and the air is cool. It's the kind of room that makes you want to whisper and tip-toe. To the right, the 75-foot lap pool and indoor whirlpool are encased in a glass room with a soaring, cathedral, post-and-beam ceiling. Straight ahead, more ocean views, which are, at once, so Maine and not Maine at all. Adjust the hue of the water to turquoise, and this could be a Caribbean hideaway. One thing is certain, though—hidden away from the outside world you are.

The first order of business is checking in. A couple of enthusiastic young people staff the desk, where personal information (how much water do I drink per day, do I have any allergies, any medical conditions?) is taken. I have arrived early so I can get my spa footing. There's much I do not know. Where do these treatments take place? Am I expected to be in the buff? Will anyone else be? These are the sorts of things one doesn't care to leave to guesswork.

I am given a key and pointed to the women's locker room, a posh and comfortable affair, where fluffy white towels are rolled and stacked like cordwood and where the showers, steam room, and sauna are located. In my locker, I find a cotton, waffley robe and "spa slippers" (disposable foam flip-flops) waiting for me. I slip into a swimsuit, don my robe, and head straight for the whirlpool. After a brief soak, I swim a few laps in the pool, making sure to keep my head above water, so as not to chlorinate my pores before my facial. I then take a seat in the spa's lounge, which, with its assortment of overstuffed chairs and couches, feels a little like an ob-gyn's waiting room, except for that million-dollar view. There's coffee, tea, and ice water available here, as well as a large bowl of fresh fruit. The gas fireplace is taking off the last of the morning's chill. This is a room designed for relaxing—and I would, if I weren't a bit anxious and excited about what was to come.

Soon, a pleasant blonde woman dressed all in white (I must con
fess, she looks a little like an angel) comes to collect me. She introduces
herself as Amanda and leads me into the "whisper zone," a corridor
lined with ten treatment rooms. I'm shown to number seven, where she
produces what looks like a white curtain, the kind you see on country
kitchen doors, and hands it to me. Except this is no curtain—there's a
Velcro fastener at the top—and I am instructed to undress, secure the
thing around me like a towel, and then climb up on the table and get
under the sheet and blanket. She leaves me alone to mull this over.

Wait a minute. I thought this was supposed to be a blueberry facial.
I had an image of sitting in a beauty-parlor chair with a bright-blue,
lumpy (and, perhaps, edible) mask on my face. Naked horizontalness
was not in my version.

Yet, a spa mentality is already starting to o'ertake me. While guests
may leave their underthings or swimsuits on if they wish, I say, what
the heck! I disrobe, enrobe, and make myself supine. Amanda returns.
My face is cleansed, analyzed ("good elasticity," I'm told), steamed, and
massaged. There's also a chest, shoulder, and arm massage. Nice-
smelling things are sprayed and rubbed on me, which, much to my surprise (usually I'm the fragrance-free type), I enjoy. Last is the blueberry
mask, and even though it is not blue, but, instead, bubble-gum pink
(only the essence of blueberry is used), I am too relaxed to care. My
fifty minutes are over in no time, and I practically float out of the ward.

After a quick lunch and a sit in the steam room (deliciously infused
with eucalyptus), it's time for my massage. Back in the whisper zone,
Don, an athletic, Canadian Mountie–looking man, takes smooth, black
stones (only one of which actually came from the cliff outside) from a
crock pot and makes two columns on my massage bed, creating a gully.
I am told to, again, disrobe and then position my spine in the gully,
which I do, and then cover myself with the sheet and blanket. I'm starting to get the hang of this.

Don returns and begins. He positions my arms over my head, my palms touching, as though I am about to do an "I Dream of Jeannie" dance. He gently pulls my wrists. Muscles I didn't know I had say, "Ah." From out of the crock pot comes a handful of baby stones, which he places between my toes. "Toe cozies," he calls them. I want to laugh and mimic "toe cozies," but I don't.

Because now, with one-and-a-half treatments under my belt, I have spa expertise, and I know the best way to enjoy this experience is to wholly give yourself over to it. You can't think, "Isn't this silly—me lying here on a bed of hot stones, with hot little stones stuck between my toes and hot stones coated in therapeutic seaweed oil being rubbed on my body?" because you will feel silly (as you probably should) and wreck the experience. No, you must let the oil and heat and hands and stones do their job (to make you feel good) and you must do your job (feel good). There have been worse things to endure.

During my fifty minutes, stones are retrieved from the crock pot. They click together in Don's hands. A stone is oiled and lowered onto a muscle. "Too hot?" he asks. I have to think. Yes, the stone is hot, but I'm not sure if it's an "ouch" hot or an "mmm" hot. By the time I have decided, the stone has cooled, the point is moot.

As a coda to the massage, Don uses a chop-chop motion up and down my back—and I can't resist: I make an "aaaah" sound, so my voice breaks into a staccato as he pounds. When he's done, I say, "I bet people do that all the time." He hesitates. "Not really."

Soon, I am nothing more than a waffle-robed wraith, gliding from room to room, in and out of this pool or that, waiting for my last treatment, the Juniper Berry Wrap, which promises a reviving and tonic effect on the nerves. Twenty-four hours ago this would have been balm, but now I have no more need for further massage than a jellyfish. How could I possibly get more relaxed?

This is how: Kathryn, a soft-spoken woman with a thick graying braid of hair and gentle manner, guides me to yet another room. I am first exfoliated with a ground-olive-pit concoction. She then gestures to a capacious stall, where the Swiss shower is housed. "Rinse off and let me know when you're done," she says, as she lets loose the spigots from an outside control. I open the doors to find twelve blasting shower heads awaiting me. It looks like a rig out of an insane asylum movie, but I'll tell you this: the Swiss know how to throw a shower.

The last step is the actual wrap itself, which involves having a lot of goo smeared on you and then being wrapped with a plastic sheet next to your skin, then a cloth blanket, then a crinkly, silver space blanket. "Now you know how a stick of gum feels," says Kathryn, as she tucks in the last fold and leaves me to steep.

By the time I'm unwrapped, I'm rubber. I'm told not to shower for as long as possible, so the goo (the juniper oils and lotions) will sink in. I am also warned to watch alcohol consumption—that my body is detoxing and drinks would go right to my head. I already feel like a cheap date. I don't think I could get much woozier.

The next morning, after a quick workout in the fitness center and a swim, it's time for my nails. Now, I am introduced to the "royal throne," an oversized recliner, with heat and massage controls for the chair and a whirlpool bath at your feet. (A stint in this would be worth the price of admission alone.) There's more massage and more wrapping of both legs and arms. The seaweed mask is the only one of the many products used on me—all for sale in the lobby, I am frequently reminded during my stay—that isn't pleasant; it actually smells like a tidal pool. Or maybe my enthusiasm is starting to wane.

I am, at last, tired of being pampered. Every inch of my body—from my cozied toes to my massaged scalp—has been prodded and kneaded like dough. I have so many scented oils and lotions seeped into my skin, I nickname myself "Sachet." As the final coat of polish goes on my nails, I begin to get antsy. I've reached the satiation point.

In the end, I figure a day visit, with just one or maybe two treatments, would've been absolutely ample. I am a Maine Yankee after all. I would've liked more lounging time. Plus, while the services are not cheap (they range between $50 and $150, excluding gratuity; nail treatments are less), they all include the use of the spa facilities, which can make for a very nice day indeed—and an excellent way to pamper your favorite Yankee, who might not make this splurge on his or her own.

And that's a value anyone can appreciate.

[2003]

Field of Dreams

Understand, I do not like to be lost. Not even mildly disoriented. I generally travel with a map in my lap. I study charts when I'm on the water. I'm so familiar with DeLorme's Maine *Gazetteer,* I bet I can tell you on which map your town is located without looking. I do not go into the Maine Mall without a guide, and I demand escorts through offices with multiple corridors and cubicles. I interrogate people about the precision of their directions. (If a poor set is given, I will not hold it against the offending party *forever,* but my regard will certainly drop.) All this can make me seem like something of a pain, but I like to be able to pinpoint my global position at every moment. It makes me feel like I'm in control.

So, you wouldn't think a maze would hold much appeal for someone like me. Mazes are, after all, purposefully designed to throw you off course, shatter your inner compass, and leave you reeling and drooling, a condition we control freaks work so hard to avoid.

But then a friend told me about a corn maze he had heard about at Treworgy Family Orchards in Levant, and I was intrigued. Although I had never before seen a corn maze, I had read about their popularity out west, where numerous small farmers—through economic necessity —have shifted away from agriculture and have, instead, opened their gates and barn doors to agri-tainment, turning their farms into nothing shy of theme parks. And at these farms, the corn maze, which can sprawl for acres and take on shapes ranging from John Wayne's head to corporate logos and often include bridges and tunnels, is considered king.

Not only did this corn-maze thing sound like a challenge to me, but I was also curious to see how the Maine version stacked up. (Even though the maze movement has been afoot since the early 1990s, it's barely taken root in Maine, where there are only a handful.) Plus, I couldn't think of a better way to spend a brilliant autumn Saturday than to coerce Husband into joining me on my lark—easy to do when the other option was chores—pile into the car, and head out on Mission Amazement.

But before we could tackle our maze, we first had to find it. Levant, for those who don't have Map 22 of the *Gazetteer* burned into the back of their brain, is located just northwest of Bangor on Route 222. That's basically all you need for directions. The orchard comes upon you suddenly, whether you're traveling east or west, but there's little chance you'll miss it, particularly on a fall weekend. Minivan after minivan crowds its parking area, which is little more than part of a flattened-down field banked by rows of squat apple trees. To gain a parking space takes some maneuvering. You may have to back up or tuck aside for the hay wagon on its perpetual route around the orchard (with stops, naturally, at the pumpkin patch). If you need to use the far-flung satellite lot, just follow the sign that says: "More parking. It's a field trip."

This jaunty attitude translates to the entire Treworgy (pronounced True-wore-gee; although they have cousins with the same name who pronounce it Tree-wore-gee) family experience, which is part pick-your-own orchard, part petting zoo, part ice cream and produce stand. The corn maze was added in 2001 as a way to help generate income, according owner Gary Treworgy. He and his brother, Dean, who is an architect, started by asking around and talking to people with corn-maze experience, since neither of them had seen one before. Dean took it from there. While most of the corn mazes they heard about out west were expansive—ten acres or more—they limited themselves to about two-and-a-half acres. According to Gary, it's been a learn-as-you-go process. Dean uses a computer to lay out the maze, but the rest is just getting out there and seeing what works. Gary says when they were in the design stages, they asked themselves: "Do we want people to come and say, 'Well, that was easy' or 'That was hard'"? They opted for the latter.

Still, it's clear their maze—like this whole farm—is targeted toward the younger set. Kids of every age roam the grounds, chasing the at-large chickens, feeding the donkey (who, according to the warning sign on his pen, bites), crunching on apples, lapping up ice cream, and carting around pumpkins. For a moment, my heart sags. Not only did we neglect to borrow a child for this outing, but I'm also struck by the fear that my corn maze is going to be nothing more than a kiddy track. Heck, my head is probably going to stick above the stalks, Gulliver style, and I'll be able to bend down, lift a tot by the straps of his Osh Koshes, and straighten out his course. We'll be through this thing, I decide, in no time.

But we've come to give the maze a go, so we take a place in line at Twig's Ice Cream Stand for our tickets (four dollars for grown-ups, two for kids, group rates for groups). When the young man behind the counter waits on us, he pauses when we request just the adult tickets, as though we're holding out on the other, younger members in our party. When we make it understood it's just us, we're given a festive map of the maze, which shows it's in the shape of an alligator (the prior year it was a kernel of popcorn), and a stamping ticket, both with the numbers one through five printed on them. We are told if we gather stamps from each of the five locations on these cards, we will receive fifty cents off the purchase of an ice cream treat when we're through. This is getting better by the minute.

We follow the signs, passing through the great barn, where more animals are housed, and emerge in the orchard's back field. From the small hill on which we stand, the corn maze doesn't look like much—a ragged cluster of stalks, really. But there's something about that cluster that suddenly seems mildly menacing. Maybe it has something to do with the bad rap that corn—as opposed to most other vegetables—has received from Hollywood. (Movies like "Children of the Corn" and "Signs" come to mind.) And why does it seem like more people are going in than coming out? And why is it so quiet? (Gary Treworgy likens being outside a corn field to standing on the edge of a still pond, with its odd noises and unknowns.) We note how warm the sun, high in the October sky, is. Should we go back to the car for water? Change into boots? Scatter breadcrumbs behind us?

At that moment, the hay wagon rolls up. The driver, Chuck, a wide-smiling guy who looks as though he's found the place he best belongs on this earth, calls down to us: "Go on, it's not that bad. We can have you air-lifted out, if it comes to that."

Chuck leaves us with little choice. All the kids who are packed into his hay wagon are now watching us. There's nothing to do but face our foe and stride into the maw of the beast.

We don't take but two steps into the entryway of corn (yes, it's as high as an elephant's eye), when a towheaded boy comes careening around the corner and almost crashes into us. The look on his face—while not exactly that of abject terror—is clearly get-me-out-of-here. He scoots by us and regains the freedom I am about to abandon. His fear is all I needed to see. The map springs up in one hand, I seize Husband's arm with the other. "Hold it," I bark. "I have to get my bearings." I scrutinize the map and develop our plan. "We'll start with station one, move on to four, then do two, three, and five, in that order." My husband, who does not possess the control-freak gene, has already disengaged himself and set off without me, with utter disregard to the map. It appears as though he has every intention of winging it. This will just not do.

As he turns the first bend, I plot ourselves on the map. That was easy enough. Another corner is taken, and we empty into a long, gently curving stretch. Good. That aligns with where we're supposed to be. The ground is dusty and littered with the occasional errant ear of corn. From within the maze I can hear muted squeals and footfalls and "wait up!"s, but the sounds are disembodied, coming from some inner sanctum, which is not yet mine. Yes, even at the onset, the corn maze is a little—forgive the pun—eerie.

Husband is the trailblazer, forging ahead, taking this all in as sport, while I constantly have to stop and re-establish our position on the map. (Just because I'm a control freak doesn't mean I'm a good three-dimensional thinker. This kind of thing—along with logic puzzles and threading a needle—gives me a stomach ache.) Eventually, we arrive at the first "station," located in a small clearing at the end of one of the corridors. In that clearing is a white stand that holds a green ink pad and a party-hat stamp, with which we mark our card. I have to say I feel a bit smug, self-congratulatory even, having taken the first station with relative ease—that is, until three giggly girls zoom up, stamp their cards, and are off in a cloud of dust and pigtails. Oh well, at least we're not lost.

For those who do lose their way, however, there is an escape path, which is bordered with red boards and runs through the center of the maze, that will quickly lead you to the outside. But using it to traverse the maze is considered bad form. In fact, a "gator memo" reads: "It is legal to cross red boards only if you want to escape the maze. Hall of Famers [those who get all their stamps and make it to the maze's center] do not cross the red boards." Not only does this path provide a reassuring safety valve, but it also helps establish your position. It's comforting to look at our map, decide we should be crossing the escape path after the next left turn, and it actually happens. It makes me feel like I'm in control.

That's not to say there aren't plenty of dead-ends and wrong turns along the way. More than once we have to backtrack. But we're not alone. We encounter one family over and over (kind of like repeatedly passing people in the aisles at the grocery store) and exchange pleasantries with the party's jovial granddad, who seems glad to be along for the ride. Shortly after collecting our number-three stamp and re-entering the circuit, a woman races up to us and says: "Is that number three? Is number three that way?" In good fun, we tell her it wouldn't be fair to give away directions. She looks at us (not so filled with fun) and pleads, "Look, I've got four kids here," gesturing to the mildly bedraggled children trailing her. We tell her she's on the right track for station three, but privately we think it might be time for a certain family to consider using the escape path.

The weird thing about the maze is that the deeper we delve, the easier it is to navigate. The map is almost unnecessary after a time. As we walk on, I feel as though I have a sense of where we should be going, as though we are being guided by some benevolent hand. I know there's nothing there, but I choose to not look up all the same.

Finally, all our stamps are collected. There's but one last step—and that's making our way to the center of the maze and the Hall of Fame, which we do with little effort. We enter the clearing, where we find a large white message board in the center with countless Hall of Famers' names scrawled all over it. We, too, pick up a marker and add our names to the board, way up at the top, out of the reach of most of our competitors.

When we finally finish, we check the time. The whole thing has only taken about a half-hour, although it seems as though we've been away longer, as if we've just emerged from not just corn, but time-warp corn. Oh well, it's nothing an ice cream won't shake off.

As we make our way back to Twig's to collect our treat, my steps are sure. I need no map to guide me. I know the way. And that's as close to finding the place I best belong on this earth as I'm going to get.

[2003]

May Migration

When I reach the juncture at which U.S. Route 1 and Route 3 part ways in Ellsworth, my car starts to drift, as if by itself, over into the turning lane for Down East Maine. This is less a reflection on my driving skills than it is my travel habits in this part of the state. To me, Ellsworth means the jumping-off point to the less-traveled "real" Maine, whereas to most of the rest of the world it serves as gateway to the wildly popular (and peopled) Mount Desert Island and its star attraction, Acadia National Park. It's been a number of years since I have, by choice, joined MDI's visitors' ranks. But I am on a special mission—I'm heading to Bar Harbor to take part in the town's Warblers & Wildflowers Festival—so I ease my car back into the proper lane and forge straight ahead.

The festival, which was started in the late 1990s, features a week of organized walks, talks, and demonstrations that celebrate the return of MDI's migratory bird population as it heads back to the island for spring feeding and breeding season. For birding enthusiasts, this return is a major event, an ornithological extravaganza. For curious novices (like me), it's an excellent excuse for stomping around in the Maine woods and, perhaps, learning something along the way.

Because it is May, and a gray May at that, traffic is light on the approach down through Trenton to Bar Harbor. Many of the tourist stops—putt-putt golf, clam shacks, T-shirt shops, soft-serve stands—are either not yet open or just recently. Motel after motel posts a sign advertising off-season rates: doubles for $28 and $35, half what the prices will likely be in a month. This stretch of roadway seems neither more nor less developed than I remember. It's just nice to be able to scoot along, instead stopping and starting behind vehicles that brake for, well, everything.

The town of Bar Harbor is all a-bustle, thanks, in no small part, to the cruise ship moored out in the harbor. It's so huge it looks fake, too big for the horizon it blocks. The streets are crowded with its passengers. People stroll along the rock-bound Shore Path and lounge in the town's grassy parks. They sip coffee drinks and pose for pictures. Despite the throngs, there are ample restaurant seats and parking spaces, and that suits me just fine. A number of businesses have yet to open. "See you in June!" say some of the signs. "Don't count on it!" I respond.

I stop by The Thirsty Whale—a restaurant and watering hole on Cottage Street popular with locals—for a fried-haddock sandwich that could feed a family of five and then head over to the Mira Monte ("behold the mountain") Inn, my home for the next couple of days. The inn is a Victorian ramble, located a leisurely stroll from town on shady Mt. Desert Street. The downstairs sitting rooms and dining room retain the feel of an age when visitors arrived by steamship and train and stayed for the summer. The staircase is lined with pictures of Gibson girls. Each guest room, which bears the name of a past grand area hotel, has been individually decorated by proprietor Marian Burns. A Bar Harbor native and former educator, Burns hosts the Warblers & Wildflowers Festival opening evening reception in the inn's parlor, saying it gives the attendees and local birders the opportunity to get acquainted. I am staying in Rodick, a sweet little room with a wee private balcony overlooking lilac bushes and the inn's abundant gardens. Even though there's a chill, I won't be able to resist leaving the balcony door ajar so I can fall asleep to the sound of the wind racing down off Cadillac Mountain.

Town is quiet at 6:15 the next morning as I prowl the streets looking for coffee. I find a restaurant open on Cottage Street, where fishermen sit on swivel stools at the fluorescent lit counter. I have one of the waitresses—a gaggle of languid and bleary-eyed college girls—fill my travel mug, and I'm off to the park for my first walking tour, "Birds at Otter Cliff."

Because I attended the festival's warbler lecture the night before and did some reading in my room, I feel a little better equipped for this experience. In fact, prior to my arrival, I could tell you exactly zero about warblers, except that they were probably going to be a lot harder to spot and identify than an osprey or eagle and that my fledgling birding skills would be put to the test.

Not to worry. Naturalist Michael Good, who gave the talk and who will be leading today's walk, has a passion for his subject that is contagious. A slim man with curly graying hair and wire-framed glasses, Good has the energetic affability of a kid's sports coach. When he describes a certain way a bird bobs its tail, for example, he bobs *his* tail. Plus, he knows this turf well. As president of Down East Nature Tours (based in Bar Harbor) and someone who has twenty-five years' experience with the avifauna of New England, he holds a wealth of local outdoors knowledge, which he eagerly shares.

Warblers, for the uninitiated, are small, (often) brightly colored, migratory songbirds belonging to the *Parulidae* family. They are very flitty, weigh about the same as a nickel, and some say they chip and buzz more than they warble. The birds have short, pointed bills and feed on insects (although not exclusively) and especially love dragonflies. They winter in Central and South America, the West Indies, Cuba, and the southern U.S., and head north when those places hit their dry seasons and food sources diminish. There are more than fifty species that breed in North America, and they often migrate thousands of miles. Mount Desert Island, which is home to 320 species of birds throughout the year, is an especially attractive destination for the warblers because of its natural diversity and the wide range of habitats the island offers. Not all will stay, however. Some species—the Canada Warbler, for instance—use MDI only as a stopover. But as I wind myself around the Park Loop Road through heavy mist and under a dense canopy of new spring leaves, it's hard for me to imagine any creature wanting to budge from this place.

Our group of ten—a woman and her two college-aged daughters, a young married couple who have been birding their way up the Maine coast, some local folks—convenes in the parking lot near Otter Cliffs promptly at seven o'clock. Good greets us, gives a bit of an overview, and then sets to work. All around us, there's the chaos of twits and chips and trills that blend into one ball of birdsong. But not to Good's aficionado's ear. He tilts his head back, lightly raises his hands, and begins naming each bird as though it were an instrument in his great avian orchestra. He gestures to his right. "Black-throated green." He cocks an ear. "There's a ruby-crowned king out there. And a hermit thrush." We follow his glances into the brush and trees around us. Binoculars are raised. "Northern parula," he says, "and a maggie" (magnolia warbler). I hear lots of chirping and see a great deal of flitting, but it's one big birdy blur to me.

We move on, wander over paths, on side roads and down the park's carriage trails, scanning the sky and the "upper canopy" (treetops) as we go. At first, we keep to ourselves, raising our field glasses when Good so instructs. (It's helpful to know your trees, since the locations are usually given as: "yellow throat, two o'clock, in the alder behind the dead spruce"—"two o'clock" meaning if the tree's top is twelve, two is a bit down to the right from there.) But at one particular stand of trees, everyone starts to get involved. Birds are spotted in rapid-fire succession, and Good identifies them as soon as they're in his sights. A local birder by the name of Ed spies a Blackburnian warbler. "Wow, oh wow, look at that orange," he says quietly. I train my binoculars on the spot and see a critter flitting around, but from my vantage point, it is hardly wow-worthy. I watch and I watch, then a flash crosses my gaze, and the bird's orange head and breast come into full view. "Wow, oh wow," I say. He's so orange and so small and the look I have of him was so hard won, I nudge Ed in the arm and thank him. We hold our positions until our arms ache.

The young married woman whispers that she thinks she sees a Wilson's warbler. Good confirms her sighting, and you can tell she's pleased. That correct identification has probably just made the couple's whole trip worthwhile. I catch the outline of a bird on a branch and bring it to Good's attention. He homes in on it and identifies it as a least flycatcher. Its dull colors are no match for the vivid black-and-yellow Wilson's, but it's my bird. He sets up his spotting scope and everyone gets a look. When we're done, he says it was a good find and asks who noticed it. Yankee modesty keeps my mouth shut for at least ten or twenty seconds, then I blurt out, "I did. I spotted it." The Wilson's woman and I exchange looks as we head back up the road. We've both now had our moment in the sun, and we bask in it.

And that feeling is precisely the goal, according to Good. He sees the festival—which he originated—not only as a celebration of the birds' return, but also as a way to introduce people to the complex environmental issues regarding development and land use, and the impact they have on these bird populations. He feels it's important for everyone—seasoned birders and novices alike—to get out in the field and experience all that diversity firsthand. "People have to be able to see the birds," he says. "Once you've identified a bird, you own it." And he's right. There's no question my bird friend now owns her Wilson's warbler; Ed his Blackburnian; and, I, my least flycatcher.

Returning to town after my morning of birding (which also included a viewing of the pair of nesting peregrine falcons and their babies in the park) is like coming home. The cold and damp have seeped under my skin, but after a tall, strong coffee and a long, steamy shower, I'm ready to set out once more. With little traffic congestion to worry about, I decide to do some exploring down toward Northeast Harbor after my day's last workshop. There I find myself alone on the utterly stunning Sargent Drive, which borders Somes Sound before slipping quietly into the residential back door of this venerable summer community. There are almost no cars, aside from landscapers' pickup trucks, and there's hardly a person to be found in a yard. It's actually a bit creepy, to tell you the truth, especially when I venture up into the surrounding high hills of Seal Harbor and see no signs of life—just a lot of driveways disappearing down and up into thick woods, driveways that almost assert, "I don't care if your car breaks down. Don't even think about venturing in here to use a phone."

It's a relief, then, to find Bar Harbor still lively upon return. On the fringes of town, children play in their yards and college kids fold their laundry at the Bar Harbor Auto Repair, Laundromat, and Car Wash complex. In the heart of town, the air is filled with the chatter of foreign accents and the click of not-very-sensible shoes. Kids whine and tug at their parents' hands. The shops are stocked with the usual plush lobster and moose toys, saltwater taffy and tourmaline jewelry, airbrushed paintings and T-shirts. But then, a turn up Main Street frames a vista of Cadillac Mountain hogging the horizon, and I remember what drew people here in the first place. A thought then occurs to me: We Mainers sometimes have it wrong about our state. We are sometimes too quick to poo-poo that which the rest of the world embraces. The birds brought me here, but this visit has been more than flashes of gold in my field glasses.

Before settling in at Miguel's Mexican Restaurant for a burrito and a Bar Harbor Ale, I pause in front of an apple tree in full-bore bloom and notice a quivering deep within its branches. It's a hummingbird. No, it's two. No three—no, more. The tree is lousy with hummingbirds. I know I must look like a dork, standing in front of Miguel's window in full view of its many diners, with my head up a tree, but you see, I now *own* these hummingbirds. And at this moment I feel a bit of ownership for Mount Desert Island, as well, and I am already looking forward to next year's migration.

[2004]

Friday Night Phosphorescence

"Once we get out there, this is going to be something like a pajama party," explains guide Karen Francoeur, who is addressing our slightly bedraggled group of eight that is gathered on a wet dock in Castine Harbor. A quick storm has just moved through the area, postponing our departure, and although we were able to take cover at the bar at Dennett's Wharf Restaurant, we are all slightly soggy. It's going on 9 P.M. There was, for a short time, a question of whether or not the outing would be cancelled, but with the night sky clearing, yawns stifled, and spirits lifting, the consensus is we forge ahead.

Our group is about to embark on Francoeur's Castine Kayak Adventures' "Friday Night Phosphorescence Paddle," which is described in her brochure as an opportunity to "[e]xplore the bioluminescent dinoflagellates"—which is a fancy way of saying we're here to look at the sparkles in the water that have entranced seafarers, beach walkers, and night swimmers for ages.

Actually, the term phosphorescence—which most of us non-marine biologist types use—is something of a misnomer, according to Tracey McDonnell Wysor, community education scientist at Bigelow Laboratory for Ocean Sciences in Boothbay Harbor. Phosphorescence, she says, refers to the delayed emission of light from an object that has been stimulated by light, as in the case of glow-in-the-dark stickers. Bioluminescence is, instead, the production and emission of light by a chemical reaction in living organisms, in this case, as the brochure states, dinoflagellates. Wysor isn't sure why we have come to call bioluminescence phosphorescence, although she notes literary writers have long used terminology like "phosphorescent seas" to describe the phenomenon, and that might be the reason. She also acknowledges when people say "phosphorescence in the water," most everyone—marine scientists included—know what's being talked about.

The term dinoflagellates, however, may require more clarification. Many dinoflagellates, she explains, are a form of phytoplankton, microscopic, single-celled, plant-like organisms that drift around (plankton being Greek for "drifter") and form the base for the entire food web in the ocean. These dinoflagellates use their bioluminescence, which is activated by a disturbance in the water, as a way to evade predators. When agitated, these tiny organisms flash a blue-green light every 0.1 to 0.5 second to attract a second predator that will, hopefully, prefer the initial predator over its prey. So, it seems that beautiful, mesmerizing marine light show is nothing more than one big display of aquatic angst.

A common myth—especially popular with sailors from the days of yore—is that the source of bioluminescence is otherworldly, resulting in the many ghost stories out on the briny blue. If you've ever seen the spectral sight of bioluminescence crashing off a ship's bow, churning in its wake, or swirling around the john in a boat's head (apparently an excellent viewing spot), you'll understand why. There is, indeed, something mystical and magical about it.

This is promising to be a real adventure, although I confess I've never been too keen about the kayak thing. On the few occasions I've tried my hand at paddling, it was only a matter of minutes before my arms tired and I started complaining. I'm also not wholly comfortable with the notion of venturing out into the ocean in a vessel that can tip over with me sealed up to my waist inside it. Plus, I must say, I've always regarded kayakers as a sort of smug and self-satisfied lot—too nouveau Maine for my taste. But because it is the assigned mode of transport to our destination, I have determined to put my objections aside and dive right in.

And Francoeur, a svelte, dark-haired woman sporting black eyeliner, is the right person to dispel my qualms. A transplanted Mainer who has adopted the state as home with a passion, she is a Master Sea Kayak Guide (which means she's guided for a minimum five years, each year consisting of at least 240 hours) and an American Canoe Association Instructor. She also has the unique distinction of being known as the "Kayak Queen of Castine," a title earned her first year in business after winning a race against a male New York Yacht Club member. She maintained her title when she outperformed the wood-fired steamboat *Laurie Ellen* after three-and-half miles. Her business, Castine Kayak Adventures, offers a full menu of outings and programs, appealing to every level of paddling experience. All of which is to say, there's good reason why she so readily inspires confidence.

Francoeur briskly takes our group—ranging from pre-teen to elder, and with zero experience to advanced—through clear and rigorous instruction before we head out. Gear—life vests, kayak skirts, paddles, safety lights, and whistles—is distributed. A brief but thorough paddling tutorial is given. We are assigned kayaks and kayak buddies (partners we will keep track of and who—hopefully—will keep track of us), and are given the all-important wet-evacuation demonstration. Francoeur is at once cheerleader and drill sergeant. She cajoles and cracks wise as she instructs, but there's a dead seriousness behind the humor. This is a fairly laid-back outing—we will not leave the harbor—but as anyone with water smarts knows, there's no room for fooling around. We all listen closely as she hammers home the importance of knowing what you're doing out there.

With the lesson done, we slide our kayaks, one by one, from the dock into the dark water and slip inside. The skirts are fastened around the opening, as though we are sealing up a bowl of leftovers. Mine is one of the first kayaks launched, and I use the opportunity to practice the stroke I have been shown on the dock. I am already anticipating sore shoulders and aching arms, but, miraculously, my craft plies the water almost without effort. I focus on keeping the blades of my paddle properly aligned and my grips the correct distance apart. Now I am using my torso and my legs as Francoeur instructed, and I'm really moving. Wait a minute. This is fun.

Once the entire group is under way, we begin navigating through the thick field of moored boats gently rocking on the tide. Castine is a famed harbor, tucked into the upper reaches of Penobscot Bay, and home to the Maine Maritime Academy. It's also one of the most venerable summer communities on the Maine coast, and the size of the plate-glass windows spilling light from houses on the shore attests to the town's wealth. But as we pass these grand homes and leave the din of the diners and drinkers at Dennett's behind, these worldly concerns gradually recede. Our safety lights, which we have attached to our life vests, bob brightly, and kayak buddies call out to one another, while Francoeur plays mother duck, making sure none of her charges strays too far from the flock. Most of us are intent on our paddling and trying to avoid crashing into each other, but then, there, shimmering in the water and around our kayaks and paddles is the first of the evening's bioluminescence. Cries and gasps and exclamations—"Oh my, oh my," "Over here!" "Will you look at that?"—go up. But this is only the start.

Francoeur instructs us to raft up for some bioluminescent dinoflagellates confab, and there is a measure of ungainly colliding and jostling of craft, like waterborne bumper cars, as we pull together, but everyone eventually gathers. One woman, Elaine, drifts toward me, and I seize her kayak and pull it into the group. Because of the dark, I can't see her face, so I don't know if I'm being forward or not. There is something uniquely strange about being with strangers in a strange environment on a strange mission in the dark. It is, indeed, something like a pajama party.

As Francoeur gives her talk, I can't keep my hand out of the water,

slowly dragging it to and fro, agitating those poor plankton that probably just want to rest. Not even the threat of having to use my newly
acquired wet evacuation technique can keep me from dipping and
swirling.

Francoeur next has us turn our lights off as we unraft and move on.
It was dark when we were in the harbor, but when we get up into Hatch
Cove, an ultra-secluded inlet tucked off the head of the harbor, it is
dark dark. Suddenly, an anchored boat appears directly ahead of me and
I have to swerve to avoid it. In these dark shallows the bioluminescence
is even thicker. Our group disperses and we become lost in our own lu-
minescent worlds. You can hear mutters and exclamations as people stir
the water with their hands and paddles. In some spots, the lights seem
to be reflecting from the ocean floor. When you get a bit of clip to your
paddling, you can see it breaking off your bow. You can hold it in your
cupped palm. Or you can just drift along and watch it blink at you.

Before we head back, we raft up one more time, to share notes on
what we've seen. Francoeur asks us what we each thought the bioluminescence looked like. It's a nice touch, forcing us, in a way, to be
poets for a moment. There's a bit of hesitation, then a voice rises out of
the dark, "Tinkerbell's wand—like at the beginning of the 'Wonderful
World of Disney.'" Next, someone says, "fire," which is followed by
"broken glass" and "sparklers." And as I listen, I'm still at it, hand in
the water, playing with stars in an upside-down sky.

When we arrive back at the dock, there's a surrealness to the bright
lights and loud voices of the late-night revelers in the bar. Francoeur
puts it this way: When she comes back to shore or paddles past people
sitting inside their yachts watching TV, she thinks, "Those people have
just totally missed seeing what we've seen. They have no idea what's really going on out here. Every time I'm out I am so glad that I was there
to experience it. As a group we've shared this awesome experience that
all these others have missed. It never ceases to amaze and energize me."

It is a sentiment, I believe I can safely say, that is shared by all of us
in our group on this evening. As we make our way up the dock, floppy

kayak skirts flapping around our legs, paddles held aloft like spears from a secret tribe, and our eyes filled with bioluminescence, I have to confess I feel just a wee bit smug and self-satisfied. It's 11 P.M., and I'm ready for bed. I know what I'll dream about. I've already seen.

[2004]

Part Two

You Want Me
To Go *Where?*

Honest North Woods Cooking

Two hundred and seventy miles might seem to some a long way to drive for dinner, but not if it's for Ken Twitchell's all-you-can-eat, lumberjack-style buffet at Pittston Farm, located in the heart of the North Woods. In fact, Pittston Farm offers such a singular dining experience people jostle over miles of dirt roads from every direction to take a place at his groaning board.

No matter your route, the drive to Pittston Farm is an integral part of the adventure. The farm lies twenty miles northwest of Rockwood and the shores of Moosehead Lake. You can approach from Greenville (I have since been told this is considered the "weenie route"), or up the very scenic Route 201 out of Skowhegan to Jackman and across Route 15. You can also travel over the Golden Road, which cuts through the North Woods, out of Millinocket. Any approach will fill your windshield with breathtaking vistas, so you should plan to roll down the windows, fill your lungs with fresh Maine air, and work up an appetite, because you are going to be *fed*.

The drive from Rockwood is over an unpaved logging road, and since Pittston Farm is located just beyond the toll booth of the Golden Road, there is a four-dollar toll in season (double for out-of-staters). As my car rumbles up and down hills and around bends, I watch for moose, deer, or any furry or feathered sighting with which I can impress my friends back in civilization, but nothing so much as a gnat crosses my view. The area, of course, is lousy with such fauna—I just assume they're all sniggering behind brush as I pass. And then, because I have nothing better to worry about, I convince myself I hear knocks and grating noises in my engine, flapping tires, and picture myself toppling into a ravine. Even though my gas gauge reads three-quarters full, I decide it is faulty and I am driving on fumes. I then try to imagine in which direction I will walk and determine how I will meet my demise: mauled by a bear, mowed down by a logging truck, wandering aimlessly into the thick woods, starved and disoriented. Because I am in the middle of nowhere. Nowhere.

Then what the heck are all these cars doing parked in the lot of Pittston Farm, I wonder, as I crest the steep hill? Who are all these people, either well-fed or wide-eyed with anticipation, milling about on the front porch and around the grounds? I feel as though I have stumbled into a lost yet teeming civilization. Where have all these people come from?

"I'm not sure," says owner Ken Twitchell, a pleasant, middle-age man with thinning red hair. "But I never dreamed I'd be feeding this many people. Never in my wildest imagination."

But since Pittston Farm opened on Memorial Day weekend in 1993, it has become something of a legend. Folks of all stripes—but with a shared lumberjack's appetite—come from all corners and over all terrains to gorge on Twitchell's home-cooked, heaping buffet.

The farm, situated adjacent to Seboomook Lake and at the juncture of the north and south branches of the Penobscot River, couldn't look more out of place deep in logging country. One expects rough-hewn log structures, not the pristine white-clapboard farmhouse and outbuildings scattered around its hundred acres, including two barns, a blacksmith shop, and a carriage house.

The area was first settled in the late 1800s, as an outpost for sportsmen. In 1906 the township of Pittston Academy Grant, including

Pittston Farm, was purchased by Great Northern Paper Company, and construction of the farm as it looks today began. It served as a base for logging crews until 1971. From 1973 to 1991 the farm was used during summers by the Boy Scouts of America as headquarters for its North Woods Adventure Program, but twenty years without either heat or maintenance was taking its toll on the structures.

And then, in March of 1992, Twitchell and his wife Sonja purchased the farm (the land is still leased from the paper company) and began the arduous fifteen-month task of restoration and renovation. Hardly new on the scene, Twitchell had served as the farm's caretaker from 1980 to 1984 and supplemented his earnings there with odd jobs that included working as bull cook for a woods crew, the influence of which is reflected in his hearty fare. The successful reopening of the farm was a dream come true for Twitchell and his wife, yet one she would only briefly enjoy. Sonja Twitchell died of cancer on January 1, 1995.

Pittston Farm is a combination inn, campground, and sporting camp (the place is jammed with hunters in the fall and snowmobilers in the winter), but it's best known in these parts as a restaurant. The main dining room, which seats about thirty, makes you feel as though you've just sloughed off your caulk boots and set down your peavey, ready for the day's big feed. Diners pass by with thick china platters piled high with a variety of meats, vegetables, mashed potatoes, homemade bread, and home-baked beans. Chairs scrape the floor, silverware clatters from the tin can placed in the center of each table, friends yell across the room to each other. It's all very homey.

There is also a long, narrow common room, all ajumble with over-stuffed sofas and chairs, a TV, and stuffed wildlife, moose and deer trophies, and animal skins. There's a gift shop and a bird room, which houses a squawking macaw, a miniature cockatoo, and pairs of love-birds. A glassed-in porch, which seats an additional thirty or so diners, overlooks the farm's pastures and offers a glimpse of the rivers.

Diners poke their heads in the kitchen door to say hello to Twitchell, who is toiling over a hot stove and overseeing the operations of the kitchen, or to call out for more meat. "Hey, Ken. More pork shoulder. I'm starving out here," calls one gentleman of some girth, clearly not starving anywhere.

Sometime after eight o'clock, things settle down some. The evening's buffet shut down and his crew fed, Twitchell relaxes briefly on the porch. What's his secret, I want to know. Why do so many people show up for his dinners in the middle of the North Woods? He shrugs his shoulders. "I have no idea." And he does, in fact, look a bit bewildered as the last of the diners clear their plates or return for one final serving of strawberry shortcake.

A food writer might term Twitchell's cooking "Yankee Regional Cuisine," but the truth is, it's the best darned home-cooking you're likely to find anywhere. A steal at $8.95, which includes the buffet, heaped with so much meat it would make a vegetarian swoon, salad bar, beverages, and desserts. Liquor is not served, although you may bring your own. An even greater steal is an overnight stay in the two floors of no-frill rooms with their spare, tidy furnishings, hand-sewn quilts, and shared bath—$40 per person, which includes three button-busting meals. The noon buffet is available only on Fridays and Saturdays in the summer, but a lunch menu is offered. The two dinner seatings are at 5:00 and 6:30 P.M.

Even if the formula is not entirely clear to Twitchell, it is one that works. The summer will see busloads of seniors traveling up from Greenville, vacationers bumping over the Golden Road, sports coming out of the wilds, a few displaced loggers, and even the occasional urbanite lining up for his buffet. Reservations are requested (via two-way radio through Folsom's Air Service in Greenville; the farm does not have a phone), but one suspects that Twitchell will always find room for you at his table. "It's always nice to know how many are coming," he says as he prepares to wrap up the day's chores. "But I'm not going to send anyone away hungry."

You can bet your lumberman's soul on that. After two meals at the farm, I feel as though I am digesting an end table as I rumble back down toward Rockwood. A deer springs in front of my car and disappears into the woods. I pause briefly, watching the animal crash through the brush, then settle back, content for the long, lovely drive home.

[1996]

Note: High gate fees on the Golden Road have severely hurt Twitchell's business. A return visit in the summer of 2003 found the place nearly empty.

Relics of the Log Drives

On a tiny island in the middle of Ambajejus Lake outside Millinocket stands something of a miracle. There, located in the Ambajejus Boom House, is perhaps one of the most comprehensive collections of river-driving history and artifacts in New England.

That the boom house, which once served as eating and sleeping quarters for the area log drivers, is accessible only by water, that the doors are left unlocked year-round, that its existence is little-known outside the Millinocket community make it something of an oddity, but hardly a miracle. What makes the Ambajejus Boom House miraculous is that it's not a project sponsored or funded by any paper company, community, or club. The concept, execution, and caretaking responsibilities were all self-initiated by one man, Chuck Harris—a veteran river man himself—who has single-handedly assembled this monument to an industry whose legacy could quite easily have slipped down the currents of the Penobscot and been lost for all time.

Cutting across the lake under the shadow of the mighty Katahdin, the rambling, white, green-trimmed boom house, so called because it was the spot at which floating logs were corralled by a chain or "boom," seems to hover before us on the water's edge. Rickety chairs sit on the porch, which runs nearly the length of the house. Scarred logs line the shorefront. Great boulders speckle the shallow cove. Harris noses the skiff onto a log landing and guns the motor, effortlessly easing the boat up into its crib. Water sloshes over the end of the sagging dock. With a packed cooler on his shoulder and a bag of groceries cradled in his arm, he steps from seat to bow to dock, setting everything rocking, but he does not so much as teeter. He's what a log driver would call "catty" on his feet.

Harris, 46, would know a catty foot from an unsteady one. He has spent nearly three decades working on and around the rivers, lakes, and dams of this once-thriving North Woods river-driving area, stretching from Canada Falls to Millinocket. But how did this experience translate into his unlikely role as advocate for the preservation of log-driving lore and memorabilia? It stems from his background, which made him just as an unlikely river man.

A Maryland native whose family summered in the North Woods, Harris studied art at the Maryland Institute and worked at the Delaware Museum of Natural History, designing, sculpting, and painting dioramas. A wiry man with wispy blonde hair and a weathered face, he speaks in an odd polyglot of Southern drawl and North Woods Yankee; his manners are courtly.

Harris first arrived to work in the North Woods in 1968 at the age of eighteen—just in time to make three river drives before they abruptly ended in 1971. He stayed on with Great Northern Paper Company, then Great Northern Nekoosa, serving as a boat operator and power-systems utility man, among other duties, until the great Georgia-Pacific layoffs of 1991.

During his first log drive he worked as a deckhand on the M.V. *William Hilton*, a 70-foot tow boat stationed on Chesuncook Lake. The training method was sink or swim, but the work came naturally to him. He confesses that from the start it felt like something he had known how to do all his life.

The river drivers were a wild, close-knit lot, he explains. They were a hard-working, hard-drinking group of men, who would risk their lives for the job, for their mates, and very often for the sake of a practical joke. Harris recounts standing on the cabin of the *Hilton,* when one of his crewmates gave him a gentle shove over the side. "I could feel the suck of the engine—it pulled a shoe from my foot—but I knew enough to push myself off the boat and swim out to safety. I've seen that engine turn four-foot logs into pulp." He notes with some pride this prank was mild for a group of men who worked in constant danger and adds, "There is no question in my mind that you could get any of the river men back out here to run logs, probably for half the pay," he says. "River driving is just something that gets in your blood. I guess that's why I never left, even when the jobs went. And I guess that's why I've put so much work into the boom house."

Harris also makes clear the distinction between logging and river driving. "I know there's a lot of documentation about logging in the state," he explains, "but the river men were a different breed. We were connected to the papermaking community, but completely separate from it. The drives had their own culture. We were the cowboys."

And it is that very culture Harris is working to preserve. Perhaps most intriguing is that he began this project in 1991, when the very industry that supported the culture he's striving to preserve put him out of work. Given the use of an old log cabin on a hill in back of the Ambajejus Boom House by his former foreman and mentor Harold Kidney, Harris began the informal task of serving as caretaker there. "By 1974, the boom house was nearly destroyed by vandals," he explains. "So Harold and I boarded it up. The furniture, which had been crafted by the river men in their off-time, had been broken up for firewood, and all the windows had been smashed out. When I arrived in '91, I knew I had to do something, so I just starting picking away at it in my spare time."

Had Harris not intervened, there is little doubt the boom house would have fallen to a point beyond repair. He first replaced the windows with whatever odd lots he could find to give him light by which to work. Slowly the rooms came to order. Cleaning, painting, repairing, or replacing the old furnishings, he gradually brought the house back to a serviceable state. And then there was the matter of collecting, sorting, and displaying the myriad artifacts. Harris accumulated most of them by scouting around the old boom houses in the area and along the shorelines. Some were given to him by Kidney, some were donated by locals. Many were brought up from the lake's bottom by divers. "There's a whole history down there," says Harris. "Any worn-out equipment went overboard. The divers told me the lake is strewn with stuff—cant dogs, pick poles, worn-out calk boots. They'd just take them off, I suppose, and hurl them out the window. When each drive ended, the men had one thought on their minds—and that was to get to town. They'd leave for the winter with enough money to get through till the drive took up again, but most of them spent it—mostly on booze and women—in a matter of a couple weeks. They lived on the street, squeezing heat [drinking Sterno], maybe trying to get thrown in jail, so they'd have a warm place to sleep and get fed. In the spring, the company would send a kid down to Bangor to round them up. Some of them would be in pretty bad shape. They'd get them back to camp and give them "the cure"—canned tomatoes and a couple beers—and in a couple of days, they would be back to the most capable group of workers you'd ever want to find."

The Ambajejus Boom House, which was placed on the National Register of Historic Places in 1973, is made up of three structures that were moved across the ice in 1906. (There has been a boom house at the head of the lake since 1835.) In the motor room, Harris has displayed the tools of the trade: tow hooks, saws, pickeroons, hawser lines, pick poles, peaveys, drift pins for pier construction, and sledge hammers are mounted on the walls; boom chains and shackles, barrels of boom plugs, and coiled lines are arranged on the floor; the sawed-off bow of an old flat-bottom boat used for the drives protrudes from a wall. But this is no harum-scarum collection. Harris has carefully arranged and augmented these displays with written descriptions (culled from his own knowledge and through library research) of how the booming operations worked, blueprints, diagrams, maps of the drives, old photos, and newspaper clippings.

The pantry is equipped with the original ice chest and food-storage cupboard. The dining room is dominated by a long table. Harris has arranged the kitchen the way it might have looked in working order, complete with vintage cooking utensils, pots and pans, canned goods, and a massive 1902 Kineo cookstove, which he transported to the island in pieces. "The cook was the boss of the area," says Harris. "The rule was 'eat and go,' so the cook could get the clean-up under way as quickly as possible." Harris tells of one of his first river-drive dinners, up at the Chesuncook Boom House. "I started in for the table, and the cook—a no-nonsense woman—put her hand to my chest, blocking my way. 'You let the older men go first,' she said. By the time I was able to serve myself, the other men were already eating their pie." He also points out that these are the only floors that aren't chewed up with spike marks from the men's calk boots. "The cook's area was a spike-free zone."

The parlor is made to depict the amenities enjoyed by the river men at leisure. Branches on which the men dried their clothes (boiled in an outdoor pot) are suspended from the ceiling by ropes above the wood stove. There are chairs and benches, cribbage boards, and books. "I don't know as though there was a lot of reading going on here," says Harris, with a sly smile. Throughout the house are paintings by Harris of river-driving scenes and various other boom houses.

Stairs from the parlor lead to the "ram pasture," where the men slept. At the head of the stairs is a painting of a pair of boots nailed to a tree. "When a man drowned," explains Harris, "there was no way to get him back to Bangor for burial. So he was taken ashore wherever he was pulled out and buried. His boots were nailed to the nearest tree—the river-man's grave marker."

The bunks were fashioned by Harris from found wood. The sloped ceilings are covered with pictures of the old crews, newspaper clippings, and photocopied selections from such texts about the river drives as Fannie Hardy Eckstorm's *Penobscot Man*. Articles of clothing the men might've worn hang from hooks. The overall effect of the entire boom-house restoration is that at any moment a crew could walk through the door and take up residence.

And that has largely been Harris's goal. It has been slow, painstaking work. Only recently has Bowater, the paper company that currently owns the boom house and the land on which it sits, expressed an interest in his project. Plans for financing a new roof, which the boom house sorely needs, are in the works. But Harris says there's still much to be done.

The greatest problem is vandalism. Even though break-ins have dropped dramatically since he has refurbished it, the boom house and Harris's cabin are sitting prey for the malevolent hand. Because he must support himself with odd jobs, he spends precious little time on the island. A donation box located in the parlor is Harris's primary means of funding his project, and even that has been pilfered.

But for Chuck Harris, these are incidental challenges to his mission to preserve a vital bit of North Woods culture. "There's not much remaining of the history of the river-driving days," he says, "but many of the people around here worked them or at least remember them. It's an important place for families to bring their kids and grandkids to show them what life was like on the river."

A history Harris hopes to continue preserving.

[1997]

Dog Days in Fort Kent

Motoring toward Fort Kent, I cross the county line on Route 11 just outside of Patten, and my journey at last begins. For, while I have already been on the road for nearly five hours, I am now entering the personally uncharted territory of Aroostook County—or simply "The County," as it is more affectionately known. I can almost feel the horizon bend and the sky widen.

The County. For two weeks prior to my departure, I savored the notion like an exotic morsel. Ashamed as I am to admit it, this lifelong Mainer, who has explored almost every corner of the state, had never ventured into Maine's northernmost county. Towns like Fort Kent, Caribou, Madawaska, Presque Isle had always conjured up notions of distant, frozen places and potatoes—intriguing, perhaps, but not enough so to make the hike from Portland. But increasingly, I had been hearing descriptions of the special charm and warmth of Fort Kent. I had been assured by those who know such things, that this particular town, located on the Canadian border, was its own experience—that it is in The County, but not wholly of The County.

Planning my trip at my desk, I gazed up at the giant DeLorme political and topographical map of Maine tacked to the wall before me. It is covered with lines of bright yellow highlighter, marking trips I had taken— spanning from Jackman to Eastport, from Baxter to Bethel. I threw my head back to see my impending destination. The County, which roughly resembles the top two-thirds of a wrench, was conspicuously fluorescent-ink-free. A visit to Fort Kent would at last fill in the final piece of the jigsaw of Maine for me.

Dodging potholes and frost heaves as I continue along Route 11, I glance in my rearview mirror and see a truck with what appears to be a rocking chair strapped to the roof of its cab. Granted, I had been on the road since early morning, and I was a little giddy. A light snow had fallen the night before, and sections of the road, which had not been cleared, are covered with stretches of slush. Between trying to keep my car from sliding off the road and my muffler from snagging off, I am not prepared for this sight on the nearly deserted roadway. When our two vehicles emerge for a moment from the thick woods lining the road, I see the rocking chair in question is, in fact, a dogsled. I relax. I realize that I am going to have a road companion for the rest of my journey. I have scheduled my visit around Fort Kent's busiest weekend—the one in which the town serves as base for the Can-Am Crown Sled Dog Races.

Arriving in downtown Fort Kent on this big weekend is the equivalent of arriving in Bar Harbor on the Fourth of July, Boothbay Harbor during Windjammer Days, or Portland's Old Port during the Old Port Festival. This is this small town's big day in the wintry sun, and its residents are in the process of going all out in preparation. I already know I am Someplace Else when I stop at Gas-n-Go Foods on Main Street to fuel up and get directions to Rock's Motel and Diner. On the gas pump, where one normally selects cash or credit purchases, there are two additional buttons: an American and Canadian flag. Up here, it's not only cash, but what kind of cash.

As I head down West Main Street, guided by the promise I "couldn't miss" Rock's, I take the leisure to look around. Fort Kent is all Main Street, U.S.A. A couple storefronts have the fakey, two-dimensional façades of a wild west town. All the action is on Main Street. From every shop window hang signs of welcome to race participants and notices of sales commemorating the event. The skinny street is already growing congested with both foot and auto traffic. As I approach the fringes of town, I see a sign proclaiming the terminus of Route 1, near the bridge spanning the St. John River to Canada. Across the street, the Rock's Diner parking lot is filled with trucks similar to the one I had seen on Route 11. On the back of each is affixed a cab with portholes, through which are thrust the heads of huskies, making the vehicles look like trophy walls on wheels.

Inside, the diner is abuzz. Sledders and mushers (snowmobilers and sled-dog racers, respectively) in great boots slog over the wet floor, which is periodically and pointlessly mopped up. Families lunch in booths, a handful of old men on swivel stools hover over coffee cups at the counter. The cook turning hot dogs and flipping burgers on the griddle, which one can openly view from the dining room, wears a T-shirt bearing the slogan, "My mind has turned to mush." On one wall is the self-same DeLorme map of my office—except this one is adhered to the wall with lots of silver duct tape and is folded so that nothing south of Millinocket shows. The County.

In front of each unit at the motel, which is set upon a rise behind the diner, is parked a sled-dog truck. Hay, scat, and kibble litter the frozen lot, where mushers tend to their dogs and visit with each other. In my tidy, pine-paneled room, I find a postcard of Rock's Motel, circa 1970. (I am guessing by the clunky sandals worn by the woman sitting on the edge of the bed with her two children atop an orange crushed-velour bedspread.) I look at the postcard, then my room. With the exception of bedding choices, it seems not much has changed at Rock's for some time, not even their clock radios.

I happily part company with my car—everything in Fort Kent is within walking distance from Rock's—and set out to take a look at the town.

Wendy Voisine is frazzled but pleasant at the Fort Kent Chamber of Commerce office. She is busy trying to find accommodations for two race participants who had not made adequate arrangements. Most of the mushers and their families are being housed by local residents. "It's just too costly for many of them," explains Wendy, between phone calls. "They need to arrive on Friday, and the 250-mile race lasts through Tuesday. So the locals help out as much as they can. We have more than two hundred volunteers involved. The town really rallies for this event." She casts a worried glance out the window at the drip-drip-drip of melt. "Just pray for cold."

I pick up a copy of the local paper, the *St. John Valley Times,* at its office, located in the rear of Nadeau's House of Furniture, and plod on. Taking a turn off the hubbub on Main Street, I find Fort Kent's fort (and wouldn't it have been disappointing if there hadn't been one?), an 1830s blockhouse situated on the bank of the Fish River. Snow is mounded halfway up its sides, and there's not a soul around. A downy woodpecker taps away at the tree behind me.

At Bee-Jay's, the town's favorite bar and a cave of a place, things are pretty un-sled-doggy at happy hour. Behind the red Formica, modified-horseshoe bar, the women bartenders gossip with the locals, sliding from French to English with gearlike ease. Along one side sit the men, Bud bottles lined before them. No microbrewed beer here. Along the other, women sip sombreros and pink cows (strawberry brandy and milk). A handful of college students (the University of Maine has a campus at Fort Kent) share pitchers of beer and shoot pool. Coolers slam open and shut. Classic rock and roll blasts from the jukebox. The only thing that anchors Bee-Jay's in the here and now is the muted picture of the TV set tuned to MTV. No one is watching.

Later, across the street at Sirois' Restaurant, the crowd is more mixed. The two dining rooms are packed to capacity with tables of four, eight, and twelve. A line snakes around the salad bar. The waitresses move with unfazed efficiency, dishing out trays of steaks and spaghetti to local married couples and families, and groups involved in the race, sporting Iditarod patches on the arms of their jackets. This is not the first busy night this staff has seen. The atmosphere is festive, but one gets the impression the atmosphere in downtown Fort Kent is always festive.

The morning of the race Rock's Diner is packed. My breakfast arrives—spoon in the coffee cup, fork slid under the eggs, toast on a paper napkin—as the town gears up for the big day.

Out on the street, trucks are finishing up laying a tract of snow along Main Street, which will serve as the race's starting point. Spectators begin to arrive, straggling in at first, but gradually streaming in. Before long, there is not a vacant spot along the race course, which runs the length of town. Friends and neighbors greet one another as they wait in line for free coffee and donuts. Tots in bomber hats bob on their fathers' shoulders. Kiddies, bundled like little Eskimos, are dragged along the street on plastic and wooden sleds. Teens in sneakers hold bare hands and try not to shiver. One mother earnestly assures her concerned child that the dogs are only happy when they're racing, that they like to pull the sleds. If every Fort Kent household is not represented at this event, it has to be pretty close.

At the grandstand near the race's take-off point, a number of local and state luminaries offer remarks. The sound of gloved hands clapping fills the air. A blessing is said, in both French and English. And then, at two-minute intervals, the sleds take off. A TV camera hovers aloft in a cherry picker. Reporters scribble in notebooks. Cameras click. The crowd, stretching the entire length of the street, cheers for each race participant with vigor.

And then it is over. The last of the sleds has slipped into the woods and fields as the race course continues out of town. And suddenly, business as usual takes claim once again over downtown Fort Kent. The trucks that had laid the course just a few hours ago set directly to work removing it. Residents head for Saturday chores and activities. Business is brisk at Quigley's True Value Hardware, as it is at Stan Albert's Route 1 Fashions.

"We thrive on snow," says the dapper Albert, as he examines a shirt a customer has placed on the counter with tie and pair of slacks. "Not this color," he says, disappearing around the corner. He returns with another shirt, holds it up with the rest of the ensemble, explains how it works better. The customer doesn't protest.

"The race is a big event for us—it makes the psychology around town better—but we have events and festivals year-round. We're a close-knit community," he continues. "This is a special place to live, there's a warmth and sincerity here you don't find many places. Just look at our downtown. We have no vacant storefronts. How many cities in the state can boast that? We all work together for what's best for the town."

You can see the truth in this statement over at Lonesome Pine Trails ("Home of the Green Bean Ski Team"), a publicly owned ski slope within walking distance of downtown. In one corner of the lodge—a modern, airplane hanger of a place, resembling a high-school cafeteria and decorated with skiing trophies—organizers from the race are tallying and posting results. But that's not where the bulk of the action is. Skiers, largely teenagers, clomp around in ski boots, balancing teetering trays of soup from the snack bar. A middle-age woman assiduously moves a broom under and around tables. Parents cluster as they wait for their offspring. A couple of mushers, quietly sipping beer at one table, check the stats when a new team comes in. A few onlookers perch on the snow bank outside at the finish line. Their cheers are thin in the late afternoon air.

En route to dinner at 7:00 P.M., I peer through the window at Bee-Jays. No milk-drink girls, no Bud boys, just one lone bartender sitting at her bar, reading a newspaper. Things are livelier when I check back later, however. The bar has filled again, and I take one of the last stools. The bartender smiles. She remembers what I drank the night before, asks if that's what I'd like, and plunks the glass down with the same, "There you go, love" as she did on Friday.

Another bartender, Lise Boucher, who has worked at Bee-Jays for twenty-four of its twenty-five years of operation, takes a moment to ponder what all those years in one bar have meant, as though it had not occurred for her to do so before. "Well, I'm now serving the kids of some of my earlier customers," she says, picking up two empty beer bottles with a quick "*Deux autre?*" as she moves down the bar.

The band is setting up in the other room. The repeated crash of drums is amplified through the sound system. Things are picking up, but no sign of mushers. Lise comes around again, and I ask her if the bar will get busy with the race people later on. "Oh, yes. Probably so. She snaps off another beer cap. "But if they don't come, the locals will come out and party for them."

The following day, I will take the long road home, across Route 1, as it hugs the St. John along the Canadian border, and down through a dull Caribou and the strip malls of Presque Isle. I will see The County as I had imagined it—rolling, empty, almost Midwestern in feel. Hank Williams songs will echo in my head.

But not tonight, not in the closed comfort of Fort Kent. After a brief turn around the now-quiet Main Street, I, at last, step up the hill toward my room at Rock's. Under the big sky, brilliant with stars that somehow feel closer up here, I notice for the first time the neon "L" in the word "motel" suspended above the building has burned out.

Yes, in this big county I do feel small. Small, but welcome.

[1998]

The Bird Man of Machias Seal Island

Beneath a bright-red umbrella, sprouting an American flag from its crest, you can find Captain Barna B. Norton guiding a group of visitors on Machias Seal Island down its craggy, slippery slope on any given summer day. The guests come to the island to view its famed bird population: arctic terns, razor-billed auks, and, especially, Atlantic puffins. Norton, 83, has come to this island—as he has for fifty-odd years—to guide birders and to maintain his claim that this fifteen acres of rock, situated ten miles off the coast of Maine, in the Bay of Fundy, is U.S. territory and, furthermore, his.

Calling Norton on the phone to make a reservation for one of his renowned puffin-watching trips is a bit like volunteering as straight man for a series of one-liners. Ask if Barna Norton is there, and you'll receive responses such as, "What's left of him" or "You're looking at him." Ask for directions, and he'll tell you, "You'll see a big sign that says California Paints. Well, you're not in California." Inquire about parking at the dock, and he'll tell you to park wherever you can, that all the spaces cost the same amount. (Parking is free.) Cite him a fact about puffins from your bird book, and he will give you a long pause and say, "Well, my puffins don't read your book." Wonder aloud how you will identify him at the boat, and he'll tell you, "You'll have money, and I'll be after it."

Norton wants your money for one primary reason: to fund his cause. As he says, "When you carry on a war, you have to have finances." The war he refers to is the Machias Seal Island war of words—whether it's a U.S. or Canadian territory—that started for him in 1940 and continues today. While Canadian-built lighthouses have stood on the island since 1832, and Canadian lighthouse keepers and a Canadian warden are the only current residents there, American officials assert a comprehensive peace treaty signed with Britain in 1783 overrides these claims—but not too loudly. This border dispute is probably the world's quietest—that is, except for Barna Norton. In more ways than one, he's kept the controversy alive and lively. "Some people have accused me of enjoying it," he says with a grin.

From his telephone banter, one expects a large person, a man of wide sails and deep seas, broad of beam. One does not expect the almost diminutive figure he cuts as viewed through the screen door of his Jonesport home. He is dressed in chinos and a festive embroidered Wild West shirt. His thin, white hair is slicked back. His face, framed by thick aviator glasses, is furrowed with crisscross lines. His socked toes protrude from sawed-off shoes. (He has arthritis; hacking off the front of his shoes provides him with relief). Yet this is a wiry, wry fellow. His step is quick, his eye is bright. No flies on Barna B. Norton. No siree.

Barna Beal Norton was born in Jonesport, June 9, 1915, the sole offspring ("I was my parents' best child") of a retired schoolmarm and an engineer for the Underwood Canning Factory. "We were poor," he says, "but we didn't know it."

He speaks lovingly, reverently of his father: "He was a teacher of many things. He loved the water and taught me that love. He was a great fisherman and was making a good living for himself before he married. My mother had more ambition for him. You could say that when he married, he lost the helm. He went to work for the Underwood Company and stayed there for fifty-two years. Back then, there were 105 sardine factories along the coast, and Underwood's was the best and most modern in the world. But it was terrible work. He made very low wages. They could get people to work for nothing. His only day off was Sunday, and we'd go fishing. He taught me a lot about the boat and the water." He pauses, casting back. "We had a lot of fun."

After high school, Norton went to navigation school in Rockland, passing in a couple months a course that was meant to last a year. He headed back Down East and did odd jobs around Jonesport, saving money to buy a boat to take him over to his island.

According to Norton, Barna "Tall Barney" Beal—his great-grandfather and namesake—had laid claim to Machias Seal Island in 1865, after the British had unsuccessfully tried to seize his vessel ("he annihilated them," he notes with obvious pleasure) and to drive the Americans away. "He began to run his fishing operation from the island, and no one dared to do anything about it," says Norton. "He was six-foot seven and something of a barroom brawler. When he died, he said the first male child that was named after him would inherit Machias Seal Island. On the day of my birth, my grandfather, John A. Beal, declared the island mine."

By 1938, Norton had put aside enough money to have a boat built, and in 1940 he launched his first expedition to his island." I took people out to picnic or to fish—people from the well-off class who summered here. I was going out to lay claim to my island. Taking people along provided the finances."

He explains that early on the puffins provided a curiosity, but were not the major draw. Gradually, however, word began to spread about these fascinating creatures, and more and more people wanted to see them. Friendly competition from other boat operators out of the nearby town of Cutler and from Grand Manan Island, a Canadian island, began. As the years passed, it became necessary to restrict the number of visitors on the island to protect the well-being of the birds. A limit of twenty-five people was agreed upon by a representative from Canadian Fish and Wildlife and the boat operators. One boat from Grand Manan would take out twelve visitors, Norton would take thirteen. The system worked smoothly for two years. Until 1971.

"That's when all the trouble started," according to Norton. The "trouble" he refers to is the Georges Bank fishing-grounds dispute between the U.S. and Canada, which resulted in a good deal of haggling and animosity between the people who worked these waters. "In 1971, the Canadians started to push to grab Georges Bank and to grab the island," he explains, getting heated. "One day around that time I landed, and the warden tried to tell me I could only take two or three people ashore. I had one answer for him—that I owned this island, that it was U.S. territory, and that he had no authority over me."

The ownership issue concerning Machias Seal Island continues to remain thorny for the two governments involved. But not for Barna Norton. Since that initial confrontation, he has spent virtually every day asserting his ownership—by marching on the island with his flag, by firing off letters and calls to government officials, by posting U.S. signs around the island and tearing down Canadian ones. He even set up a territorial council to govern the island, one he himself has described as "the most disorganized outfit you ever saw."

Beyond ownership, however, Norton has but one main concern, and that is the protection of the birds. He is particularly irked by researchers, whom he sees as vandals: "The University of New Brunswick has all those molesters out there, studying the birds," he says. "They don't need to study the birds. When the little puffins come out, they chase them all over the island and band their legs." To prove his point, he produces two photographs. One shows a hale and hearty puffin; the other, a banded one, with a deformed leg. He pauses. "My question is, wildlife people protect the birds from the public. Who protects the birds from the wildlife people?"

One might not understand this passion without a visit to the island, to which Norton brings between 500 and 800 guests from all over the world each year. On this particular summer morning, thirteen passengers have found their way past the California Paints sign in the sleepy seaside village of Jonesport and are assembled on the dock by 6:45—per Barna's instructions. The serious birders are easily distinguished from the merely curious. Dressed in sturdy shoes, pants, and warm jackets, with high-tech binoculars and expensive cameras dangling from their necks, the birders have a reverential air. A trip to Machias Seal Island, for them, is a grand pilgrimage. A young couple—novice birders, if birders at all—huddle over Styrofoam cups of coffee and shiver in T-shirts and shorts, but they seem equally excited. Threading his way through the group, Barna Norton collects cash and checks from his passengers, bantering and slinging one-liners all the while, as his son, John, tinkers around in the cabin of the 30-foot *Chief*.

John Norton, 50, shares his father's zeal for protecting the puffins and maintaining the claim to the island. He cuts the figure of a seaworthy salt. His face is weathered, his nose looks like it might have been broken more than once, and he moves, his black jeans tucked into waders, with the assurance of someone who knows his way around the water. In regards to protecting the birds, he says, "I've been coming out here since I was five years old, and I've seen these waters change. Knowing what not to do to the birds is half the battle. And I know what not to do."

But it is also clear he knows what *to* do. He is swift and deft with lines and gear. Once at sea, and with his father at the wheel, John takes time to stroll about the deck, answer questions about the wildlife ("that's John's department," says Barna), point out birds and sea creatures, and offer historical information about the area. Looking one visitor dead in the eye as he answers her question, his arm suddenly shoots out, pointing. "Sooty shearwater," he says, without so much as a sideways glance.

As the boat approaches the island, a miraculous phenomenon takes place. Flapping madly in the air is a lone puffin. (No bird has ever looked so much like a cartoon of itself.) Then two puffins. They come, as a snowstorm comes—one flake, one bird, at a time—and then whoosh—you're in a big swirl.

And then there's the island, which, on approach, looks like a quivering white heap. It is, in fact, lousy with birds. Guests are ferried, via dory, by John to the island. With no dock, they must scramble, with the help of the lighthouse keepers and the warden (the Nortons are and always have been on good terms with these Canadians), over slippery rocks and up a decrepit ramp. Sticks are made available to hold over their heads to deter terns from dive-bombing. When all have assembled, Barna pops up his umbrella, American flag fluttering pointedly atop it, and leads his charges to the spectacle they've been waiting for.

Hoards of puffins, razor-billed auks, Arctic terns, and a scattering of common murres perch and strut everywhere. All are struck by the sight. The passengers are split up by the warden, who ushers groups of three into various blinds strategically sited around the island. This is not glamorous stuff. The blinds have all the ambiance of an outhouse (replete with the strong smell of nitrogen), and you are expected to remain in your blind until the warden comes to fetch you a half hour later to switch blinds.

But those with an eye for birds—and even those without one—don't seem to mind. The birds come so close, you could reach out and touch them. You can hear them land—oomph! (puffins do not have graceful landing gear)—and claw across the roof. The half hour flies.

So how will the issue of Machias Seal Island ownership be resolved? Perhaps it won't. In the meantime, Barna says that he will try to get recognized as the owner of Machias Seal Island, will cooperate with the Canadians, but will also march on his island with his flag just as long as he is able, and, finally and emphatically, he will continue to do everything he can to protect the birds.

As he says, "Without the puffins, we've got nothing but a bald rock out there."

[1998]

Mackworth Island Interlude

December dusk falls hard on Mackworth Island—but not all at once, and not all in one place. For me, the allure of a late-afternoon winter visit to this 100-acre island located a half-mile off Falmouth is part beat-the-clock challenge, part the kaleidoscope of light and shade, and part the almost assured fact I will have the place largely to myself.

Even for the non-sporting type (me), winter in Maine—the bony spinster of our seasons—has its particular, albeit austere, appeal. Time slows. The landscape, devoid of bugs, crowds, and foliage, gives way to a stripped-down beauty. In this spare environment, you can see things more clearly. Thoughts unclutter. Sometimes you can even forget it's cold.

As I cross the causeway to the island, the light almost instantly changes. The air becomes achingly clear, the water glistens, the sky is a cornflower blue. For years, I have relied on a trip to Mackworth—just a few minutes' drive from Portland—to bust away the cobwebs and shake off the city dust. The mile circuit around the island is an economical retreat. If I need but a quick turn in the woods and glimpse of the ocean, I can have it in the time it takes me to do my dishes, over which I rarely linger. But it's hard not to dally once I'm on Mackworth.

And, no doubt, this is what former Governor Percival Baxter had in mind when he made a gift of the island, his family's summer home since 1885, to the state in 1943. He stipulated this migratory stopover for birds be maintained as a wildlife sanctuary and used solely for public purposes. Ten years later, when the state legislature was considering appropriations for a new campus for the Maine School for the Deaf, Baxter offered $500,000 to locate it on Mackworth Island, to which he later added an additional $200,000. The school officially opened in 1957 as the Governor Baxter School for the Deaf.

Even in winter, the school and its outbuildings, sited within stands of tall pine and spruce on the center of the landmass, rarely come into view from the level of the nature trail that circles the island. The only structure most visitors see is the shingled gatehouse at the end of the causeway. No fees are collected, there are no requests to declare contraband. Occasionally you can be turned away—parking is limited—or be reminded the trail closes at sundown. The daylight is waning. I get a move on.

Choosing the counterclockwise shore route, as is generally my wont, I find the only sign of humanity is on the horizon. Before me are the familiar sights of Casco Bay: Spring Point, its breakwater and stubby lighthouse; Fort Gorges rising from a hunk of ledge in the bay; and, in the distance, a shadowy silhouette of Portland Head Light. Portland's Eastern Promenade and the South Portland waterfront can also be seen. Frozen in this light, the scene looks like a diorama.

A tree-topped cliff to my left towers over the beach, which is a strip of snow, strip of sand, strip of ice, strip of sand. The light cuts hard in my path. Even the smallest pebbles embedded in the beach cast long shadows. Fallen trees line the shore, some covered with deep green moss, some bleached blonde and ashen. The terrain beneath my feet changes radically and often. I move slowly through soft sand; I crunch over mussel shells and feel like I'm walking on broken china; I climb over rocks and slip on ice; I slog through muck, my boots making a smacking sound with each step. My jacket swishes as my arms swing back and forth. For such a quiet place, a lone traveler can make a lot of jacket in winter.

Yet, when I stop, white noise prevails. The inky-black water on the shore gently slurps. There is a dull hum of semis on I-295, the whine of a small plane far aloft. And then I round another bend, and quiet. Around me is the dull palette of winter: wheat-colored sea grass, exposed rock of patina-green, oxidized rust, rosy quartz, golden moss. Yet, the usual mix of summer smells—the tangy salt air, sweet pine, the fecund or fetid aromas of marine life and death—are notably absent. All I smell now is the occasional whiff of aloe from the swipe of a Kleenex.

Approximately halfway around the island, a long stone pier juts out into the water. At its end, the islands in the bay crowd into my view, but the horizon still feels open—like on a clear day, I could see forever. A small duck bobs in the water below. "Hey bufflehead," I call, for no reason but the sheer pleasure of uttering the word.

From this point, as always, I leave the shore to finish my walk along the bosky interior path. The tide right now is high, and the going can get tricky. Besides, I am here as much for turf as surf. Access to the shore can be easily had later on, if I so choose.

Rounding the east side of the island, the light suddenly ends. Just like that. Stones and trees go flat. The subtle hues are drained from the landscape. The tableau before me becomes a monochrome—perfect dreariness for scooting into the woods to the island's famed burial ground. There, beneath a canopy of cathedral pines, within a circular stone wall, you'll find deceased Baxters aplenty, but not of the human variety. This graveyard is for the Governor's beloved dogs, as well as Jerry Roan, "a noble horse and kind friend," who left this world in 1904 at the age of thirty-five years. A large boulder stands at the graveyard's center, studded with commemorative bronze plaques. One states Baxter's other stipulation when he gave the island: "The State of Maine by Legislative Act Chapter I, Laws of 1943, accepted the gift of Mackworth Island and covenanted to maintain forever this burial place of my dogs with the stone wall and the boulder with the bronze marker thereon erected in their memory. Percival P. Baxter."

Elizabeth Peavey

A crow cackles overhead. In the gloaming, the trunks of pines glow red. Something—a clump of snow, a pine cone, a canine spirit—suddenly crashes through the limbs and sends me fleeing for the path, sufficiently spooked.

My feet follow the familiar treads of Bean boots and sneakers as I round the last bend on the island. Others have recently been here before me, but I've encountered no one. The wind kicks up, and my face starts to stiffen in the cold. The last rays of daylight stream through gaps in the thick woods and wash the shore and islands in the distance orange. I make a hairpin turn on the path, where, before me, lies a large snow-covered meadow, and the slightest glimpse of the school—a signal my brief retreat is coming to a close. As I approach the causeway, the sun blinds. On the shore below, slabs of ice heap up like scales. Early night is coming on. I've beat the clock one more time.

As I pass by the gatehouse, I'm almost glad to see another human again. No, I did not entirely leave civilization. It only feels that way.

[1998]

Rangeley Retreat

Deep in the heart of the Maine winter, while friends are packing their swimming togs and setting their sights on points south, I opt for a different sort of winter warmth. What I want is *away*. Away, on its own will do. Thus, I look to the western Maine mountains and, in their midst, Rangeley.

Let me be clear. What I am seeking is not an embrace-the-great-outdoors getaway. As I load my car, there is nary a ski, snowshoe, or skate to be seen. The closest I come to gear is a fully stocked book bag and a bottle of nail polish. I may not be the only person who has ventured to the North Woods in winter with a plan to paint her toenails, but I'll bet I'm the first to admit it in print.

Motoring north from Portland, my traveling companion and I have chosen perhaps not the most prudent course into Rangeley—Route 17—but what's a muffler between friends, after all? The going is slow, but the country is open and hills surround us. The roadway is a vast ribbon of undulating frost heaves, some marked, some not. You quickly learn when you see a blaze-orange "Bump" sign on Maine's back roads, they mean it.

"Away" is finally achieved when we cross into the township of Letter E. When I first saw the sign, years ago, with its vertical stacked letters, I thought it was a French town, *Lettere*. Since then, it has served as a gateway for me. When you enter the land of lettered townships, you know you are somewhere else.

Slowly the car climbs a stiff, winding grade. And then we reach Height of Land. No place in the state is so aptly named—you find yourself literally on top of the world. Rimmed by mountains that stretch to the horizon, Mooselookmeguntic Lake sprawls in a deep dish below. A brief scramble up a snowbank to take in the view, however, is quite sufficient. It's cold up here.

As we approach the town of Rangeley, we catch a look of Rangeley Lake and the frontierlike village. Shops and restaurants cluster together on Main Street. We pass Stubby's convenience store, dozens of snowmobile crates stacked up in piles in storefront parking lots, and not one single outlet shop. At the end of the village, a massive, three-story, blue-shingled structure dominates a bend in the road. We have finally arrived at the Rangeley Inn.

I must confess, no matter how many times I stay at lodging houses, I always feel a sense of childish excitement when checking in. It's like the first day of school, without the dread. You wonder what your room will look like, where it's located, what the view will be. I see other guests who already have the lay of the land, coming and going with purpose or settled into their favorite lobby chair—they have senior status to my freshman goofiness. I know this anticipation will be fleeting, so I pause for a moment to enjoy it and look around.

The Rangeley Inn, which dates back to 1907 and has been lovingly restored over the years, is at once cozy and campy and elegant. The most distinguishing feature of the columned, dark wood lobby is a giant moose head mounted on the wall over a stone fireplace (disappointingly gas-fueled), which is flanked by an antique sleigh and a grand piano. An old wooden (working) phone booth is tucked at the foot of one of the two staircases; wing chairs and an overstuffed sofa offer ample lounging room. It's all so inviting after the long drive that I want to drop my bags then and there and flop down with a book, make a phone call, and play "Chopsticks." No need to rush things, I decide. I have the whole weekend in front of me.

As I make my way to the old-time reception desk, the floor creeks beneath the plush burgundy carpet. I rock on one spot just for the pleasure of its music. Things are busy—it seems we're not the only ones on retreat. The phone rings, guests wait for local information or to make dinner reservations. The receptionist handles it all deftly and pleasantly. I'm not even in a rush to get my room key. Already, the vacation is taking hold.

While the inn includes a modern motel unit out back on Haley Pond, the main lodge's rooms offer more unchanging pleasures. Each is unique, updated with modern baths, some with claw-foot tubs, many with restored oak furniture and flowery wallpaper. Our room has a large walk-in closet—perfect for tossing bags and closing the door. Perhaps I'll unpack later, if I get to it, but now is the time to get down to the business of some serious relaxing.

Afternoon unspools into evening, and I already feel like I own the joint. Earlier, we examined the antique photographs of Rangeley displayed throughout the inn, stopped for a brief sit in the TV room located off the lobby, and then settled by the blazing fire in the inn's tavern and watched the parade of sportspeople return from their day in the wilds. Snowmobiles sputter and roar outside at all hours, but things simmer down considerably when dark descends. Helmeted women, men, and children clomp around in their heavy boots and snowsuits. One woman, with a sharp Massachusetts accent, complained to her husband about the cold. "We stayed out too long," she said. "I have no feeling in my toes." This was clearly the husband's fault, and he is duly chagrined. As for us, we haven't set foot outdoors since our arrival. All our toes are warm and accounted for.

On this Saturday night, the adjacent dining room is hopping. Long tables filled with parties of six and eight dominate the center of the dining room, while couples and small families occupy tables around the fringe. The wood floors and wainscoting are so thick with varnish they seem almost liquid under the chandeliers' glow. And the high tin ceiling, painted a shade a quarter-to-Pepto Bismol-pink, bounces back the sound of lively conversation. The efficient waitstaff whisks around the dining room and chats with the diners. All this activity after so much laziness makes me feel almost invisible. Happily.

We take our time through dinner—it's not like we have to rush off to a floor show here—and linger over coffee. We are seated beside the room's great front windows. Every so often, a car passes along Route 4—but only every so often. The food and sloth have caught up with me. I'm sleepy. Time to call it a day.

In the morning, however, I am filled with resolve. That is, after I sleep in to an hour that would make my Yankee ancestors shudder with horror. I pad down to the lobby in stocking feet and unkempt hair and help myself to the complimentary coffee, while I make my plan. This will be the "outdoor" day, I decide. Not that I intend any form of physical exertion—I haven't completely lost my mind (nor do I intend to lose any feeling in my toes)—but there's a town to see and some nature to be gawked at.

I start by spending an inordinate amount of time gearing up for a walk through town. A quick gloveless run to the car leaves my hands looking like flank steaks. By the time I am finished swaddling myself in fleece, Gore-Tex, and wool, I look like the Michelin Tire Man. My companion will not dislodge himself from his chair or his book for this part of the adventure. I waddle to the lobby, solo and ready to seize the day.

As I pass through the inn's doors, the cold of the day does not so much slap my face as adhere to it. I can almost hear my skin and my lips cracking as I make my way down the street, which is surprisingly peopled. Outside Doc Grant's Pub, a sign boasts that Rangeley is halfway between the Equator and the North Pole (3,107 miles to each) and at an elevation of 1,547 feet. I poke around antique and gift stores, with names like Moose America and Loony Moose, which are stocked with souvenir moose T-shirts, bookends, and dishtowels. Side by side with all the tourist places, however, are regular small-town businesses:

the IGA, the hardware store, real estate offices, the movie theater. Inside the Rexall drug, townies make up most of the clientele. A friend of the cashier gossips as she waits for a prescription for the baby slung on her hip. I have stopped in only to get warm. I buy some lip balm on a whim—another extravagance in the eyes of my ancestors; I have some, somewhere, in one of my bags—and comment on the cold. "Oh, it's warming up," I'm cheerfully told. "It was ten-below when I came into work this morning."

The bulk of the afternoon is spent seeing if I can't dislodge my muffler once and for all. Pried from his now-favorite lobby chair, my companion has joined me, and we bump over to Oquossoc—a rough-and-tumble little lakeside community, sited at the head of Mooselookmeguntic, with a country store, a tavern, a couple of restaurants, and sledders galore. The town's laundromat bears a sign: "Frozen. Closed for the season." At the boatyard, watercraft are stowed in units resembling giant post-office sorting boxes. We see Route 4 to its end— at Haines Landing—and find quiet. Camps and cottages crowd toward the shore, but most of them are buttoned up for the season. The lake, snow-covered, sprawls before us. The winter sky is wide and dazzling.

From Oquossoc, we head for Moose Alley—Route 16 between Rangeley and Stratton—a road that is all woodlands and mountain vistas. I try my moose call, "Here moose. Come 'ere boy," to no avail. At one point, we see a car stopped in the middle of a straightaway: a North Woods signal that there's probably something worth looking at. We slow, too, and see a doe grazing. For a moment, we share this twilit pleasure and then press on.

It's now Sunday night in downtown Rangeley, and with most of the snowmobilers departed, things have quieted some. We stop at a local pub and have no trouble finding a seat. A few regulars nurse beers at the bar; families gather in the dining room. The stereo blares hits from the '70s. We have a quick refreshment and then make our way to an early dinner at the Country Club Inn, located just on the outskirts of town.

In the large lobby, twin fireplaces face each other from opposite ends of the room. Paneled walls, mismatched sofas and chairs, coffee and end tables—and, yes, the ubiquitous mounted moose head—make for a campy, rustic atmosphere. We idle in front of the fire before taking our table in the glassed-in dining room, which, by day, offers stunning views of snow-covered Rangeley Lake, Saddleback, and other mountains looming in the distance. Being a borderline pyromaniac, I get the urge to poke at the logs (in my mind, all fires require fixing), but a framed poem on the mantelpiece, beginning with the line, "If it's warmth that you desire/poke your wife and not the fire," dissuades me. Later, when I mention the poem to the innkeeper, she laughs and shakes her head. "Oh, we don't really mean that. We just don't want people stoking the fire late at night and then going to bed. But people love the poem. We get requests for copies of it all the time."

After dinner, we wander downstairs, where the Country Club Inn's motel-style rooms are located. The paneled halls are lined with framed tourist brochures of yesteryear. It strikes me: all this nostalgia, here; and all around Rangeley—which, after all, has been a retreat for rusticators since the mid-nineteenth century—seems genuine. I get the feeling that the comforts of the area are timeless and lasting, and those who preserve them and visit here are happy to keep it that way.

In the morning, we savor the last of our stay at the Rangeley Inn, which now feels like home. We wander downstairs for a hearty breakfast and then make a leisurely departure, descending the winding roller coaster of Route 4 out of town.

No, when I get home, I will not have to shake sand from my bags; nor will I have a suntan. I will simply return with the feeling that I have truly been away for a spell. And that feeling, plus my newly painted pink toenails, is going to be enough.

[1999]

Holy, Holy, Holy

"You'll find it," was the basic gist of a friend's directions to the South Solon Meetinghouse, as though divine intervention would lead me to my destination. And yet, I have my doubts as I head off Route 201, northwest of Skowhegan, in the heart of Maine's farming country. After a wrong turn or two, I approach a crossroads I cannot locate on my trusty DeLorme. Just when I think all is lost (oh me of little faith), the white clapboard building appears, sitting primly fringed by woods and flanked by field. It comes upon me so suddenly, I feel more like the meetinghouse found me than I found it.

Any wayward traveler might, too, be struck by the sight of this stark 1842 structure plunked in the middle of nowhere. Typical of rural colonial-style houses of worship of its time, it is a study in understatement. Aside from the square bell tower adorned with finials and the soaring miter-topped windows, there is not a hint of decoration—no shutters, no columns, just a plain rectangular box. The austere exterior suggests simplicity and economy. As it turns out, this façade is nothing but a poker face and does anything but prepare the visitor for what's within.

As I unlatch the hook-and-eye lock, I instantly understand how Dorothy must have felt when she opened the door of her black-and-white farmhouse into the land of Technicolor Oz. Before me is a tempest of color. The contrast from exterior to interior is so startling, it is at first difficult to focus. All I can see is that every inch of wall and ceiling looks as though it's been draped with a gigantic eccentric quilt. The colors are so soft, the surfaces seem like they would give to the touch. When I regain my wits (no small feat even under normal circumstances), I see that this riot of color is, in fact, not pliant, but plaster-hard. The interior of the meetinghouse has been decorated with other-earthly religious frescoes depicting Biblical scenes and figures. The sanctuary itself is structurally plain. There are rows of boxy numbered pews with doors; a modest, raised pulpit; and a second-floor gallery. Light streams in from the tall windows through wavy panes of glass. The quiet is almost palpable. And then there's all that color. The combined effect is—to borrow from the vernacular—holy, holy, holy.

This meeting of the ascetic and the aesthetic is in itself an unlikely phenomenon. That it is located at such a distant outpost heightens the intrigue. And yet, how it came to be is the simple story of what happens when a small community joins forces for a common good.

The South Solon Meetinghouse and its frescoes, which were painted through a program at the nearby Skowhegan School of Painting and Sculpture, have a long-revered history in this tiny hamlet, according to Joan Franzen of the South Solon Historical Society. "The building is widely used by the community for weddings and concerts, or just as a place of private meditation," says the slender, older woman in her home in Solon. She also adds that despite its remote locale, thousands of people from all over the country visit the meetinghouse each year and many send donations. Franzen should know: She is a historical society of one and has a long familial interest in the meetinghouse.

According to *South Solon: The Story of a Meetinghouse,* published by the South Solon Historical Society in 1959, the meetinghouse was constructed by members of the First Congregational Church of Christ ("church" then referred to a group of people, not a building) by and for the congregation. Yet while it was "consecrated to religious devotion," it was also meant to serve as a "center of community life of every kind"—a goal that has been realized throughout its rich history.

The meetinghouse remained vital through the end of the nineteenth century, until industry drew families away to cities and farming waned. It began losing its constituency and, by 1904, services were abandoned. For the next thirty-five years, it sat idle.

And that's when Franzen's parents, Willard H. and Helen Warren Cummings, stepped in. "My family rescued it when it was falling down," says Franzen, whose brothers were also active in the community. (King Cummings was one of the Skowhegan School's founders.) "They bought the meetinghouse for fifty dollars, and we had a church raising." The community jumped in, the first service was held in 1938 (actor Vincent Price came from the neighboring Lakewood Theater to read Scriptures), and repairs began immediately. Religious services resumed and educational programs were instituted. The South Solon Meetinghouse was born again.

Of course, the restoration of the physical structure tells only half the story. In the 1950s, the meetinghouse took on another new life. Through the Skowhegan School, a program was set in place in 1952 to decorate the meetinghouse walls with frescoes—a technique in which paint is applied to fresh, wet plaster. Based on sketches submitted through a national competition, three Margaret Day Blake Fellowships were awarded each year for five years to young artists by a juried panel. Selected faculty and students from the Skowhegan School were also invited to participate. The artists were, for the most part, given free rein, but were asked to bear in mind the religious character of the building, the scale of the space, and to work in harmony with each other.

The results of this project are what meet the eye at the South Solon Meetinghouse. Though the murals widely vary stylistically, there is a sense of a larger picture. The Old and New Testaments serve as the primary subject matter. Catholic, Jewish, and Protestant religions are represented. Tom Finkelpearl, director of the Skowhegan School, notes, "What makes the murals so interesting, is how multicultural they are, particularly for the 1950s. One of the founders of the school was Jewish and was responsible for much of the Old Testament work, and the ceiling was painted by an African-American." He also points out that these frescoes were not a fluke, but part of an ongoing program that remains alive and well today.

Yet—as with most works of art—all this background is not necessary to appreciate the South Solon Meetinghouse's beauty. In fact, the uninformed visitor might be the most appreciative—or at least most awed by the sight. But for those who require answers and explanation, there is a framed guide to each panel, in which the subjects and artist are named, located inside the meetinghouse.

In the narrow foyer, a guest book sits on a rickety table next to a rusted coffee can containing a few bills and a scattering of change. In the spiral-bound notebook are inscriptions—ranging from children's blocky hand to elders' spidery scrawl—with an overwhelming plaint: "Be good to this building."

In case anyone has ideas to the contrary, a semi-circular wall in the foyer depicts the early forefathers of the meetinghouse and others who played a role in its restoration. The figures almost seem to stand sentry. Franzen says the fresco (which was painted by her father) was inspired by a photo of the church elders found in the meetinghouse attic, "along with a number of empty rum bottles."

As I enter the main sanctuary of this eminently simple building, a massive Godhead seems to bear down on me in deep, earthy colors from the ceiling. Directly behind the pulpit is an explosion of light and trumpets, surrounded by rain and waves. A human-looking angel takes clumsy flight. To my right, tortured figures contort in pain. This north wall is all dull color, edges, and angles—very Old Testament. To my left, a less grim palette prevails. Soft, heavenly light falls upon a number of scenes. In the rear corner is a depiction of the Last Supper. Toward the front, little flames dance out of the heads of Apostles. Behind me, on the east wall's center panel, figures are painted in thick, fingery colors. Above, in the gallery, a chorus of angels clutches musical instruments—

a winged orchestra. No matter where my gaze lands, a new detail or image can be found. The effect is dizzying. After a time, I am so over-whelmed, I don't know whether to make a joyful noise or crawl under a pew in repentance.

As I mount the creaky stairs to the gallery for one last look around, it is with a true sense of ascension. This elevated view gives yet another perspective on the scene. Light seems to cascade down the walls, and it is difficult to tell if paint or actual light is at play. From a distance, the Old Testament figures seem less menacing, the explosion behind the pulpit less violent. On the south gallery wall, a muscular angel wrestles with Jacob in a tangle of limbs and wings. On the opposite wall, tucked in a dark corner, an ark is tossed by waves. A dove hovers with an olive branch in her bill. It is one of the smallest, simplest panels and yet, to me, the most hopeful.

I have found what I came looking for at the South Solon Meetinghouse, and I leave refreshed.

[1999]

Mapping Matinicus

Matinicus Island, which is located twenty-three miles from the mainland in the outermost reaches of Penobscot Bay, is something of a mystery. Though very much a Maine island, it couldn't be farther flung from the-way-life's-meant-to-be Vacationland congestion and commerce that clog the coast. While there are a number of rental cottages, and the island's sixty or so residents (this number shrinks in winter) seem to host a parade of guests, tourism is not a big part of the Matinicus economy. There's only one place to stay, Tuckanuck Lodge, which is more boarding house than upscale inn. There's just one restaurant/general store, and its hours are limited. Unless you have your own boat, travel to and from can be costly or inconvenient. (The ferry from Rockland serves the island just three and occasionally four times per month from May to October; air travel is $35 per person each way.) Oh, yes, and the Matinicus chamber of commerce has an annual operating budget of $50. It's not like they're falling over themselves to get you to come visit.

Nor does Matinicus bear much resemblance to its island neighbors. It boasts neither the grand manses of Vinalhaven and North Haven, nor the summer artist colony of Monhegan. It generally lacks the misty-eyed romantic aura most Maine islands possess. In fact, its mainland reputation—for the few who know anything about it—is as a hard-scrabble, rough-and-tumble fisherman's island, where things haven't changed much since its settlement in the mid-eighteenth century. Even its name, meaning "grassy isle," is sharp-sounding, especially when you compare it with islands such as Little Cranberry, Wooden Ball, or the jaunty Junk of Pork.

So, what's the appeal? Perhaps these very qualities. Matinicus is simply all authentic Maine island, all the time.

From the outset, Matinicus makes a bold impression. The ten-minute flight via Telford Air from Owls Head is like soaring over an Eric Hopkins painting; the jagged rocks and verdant islands lay flat in the green-blue water below. The pilot circles and then quickly makes his descent. He bumps the plane up the spruce-lined dirt air strip, and you and your gear are discharged at the "Matinicus International Jetport," a ramshackle structure that was perhaps a one-time tool shed or abandoned outhouse and in which you can be sure you're not going to find a Hertz rental counter—that is, if you could enter, which you cannot, since it's filled with banana boxes. The prop is fired up again, and the pilot is off. The whine of his engine gradually fades, and then you find yourself absolutely, exquisitely nowhere.

All this happens so quickly, it leaves you reeling. The stillness of high August, the sweet scent of fir, the towering spruce are hypnotic. Time slows; it's easy to cast back to another era. Was it a plane that just brought you here, or was it a properly trimmed dory and a freshening wind?

The first leg of the mile-long trek to the lodge does little to dispel your reverie. From the airstrip, you pick up the island's main road, which runs north to south and divides the island, which measures two miles long and a mile wide, in half. Another road crosses the island at its center, east to west, creating four quadrants.

As you trudge along the sun-baked dirt road, you pass pristine Capes and farmhouses (agriculture, once a mainstay here, ended around the Depression) that gleam white in the island's Edward Hopper light. The lawns are neat, to the point of being manicured, and the flower gardens and occasional vegetable patch are well-tended. But there's not a sign of life—not a person, not a dog, not a car. There's only the arc of blue sky overhead and the distant grind of a lobsterboat.

Things liven up, however, as you approach the four corners and Matinicus's hub. At these crossroads stands the island's trim church, with its modest steeple and bell tower. Beyond it, is the old school, a traditional New England–style meetinghouse, which is now occasionally used for a gift shop, a farmers' market, and other public functions. Adjacent is the new school, a modernish structure that looks like most any elementary school, except wee.

Heading east from this intersection, the road diverges in a number of directions. Where the north road felt open and endless, here you are at once closed in by towering fir trees and the tangle of greenery, wild raspberries, and purple fireweed that bank the road. A bicyclists bumps past. A car—its rear passenger door replaced with plastic sheeting and duct tape—rumbles by. A woman struggles with a giant black suitcase she is dragging on its useless wheels over the dirt. She might as well have the words "NOT FROM HERE" tattooed on her forehead.

A sharp and then a soft right brings you to Tuckanuck Lodge, a modest shake-shingle Cape set back from the road. Its five reasonably priced rooms, which include breakfast, are clean and comfortable. Proprietor Bill Hoadley, a spry and wiry man in his early sixties (he actually *runs* while mowing the lawn), is a welcoming host. He'll regale you with his catalog of island yarns and point you toward good places to see and explore.

The truth is, you can take in most of Matinicus in a day, but that would be missing the point. The greatest appeal of this island is the opportunity to slow down enough to suspend a moment of summer, and to remember what August in Maine is all about. Most of the island— save the northeast and southwest rocky ledges—can easily be traversed by foot; there are no steep grades and good walking trails are abundant. Don't expect to find trail markers, white slashes, or cairns, however.

Hoadley provides his guests with a map with the following disclaimer: "This map may be inaccurate, but we cannot guarantee it. Some trails may have disappeared through dis-use." It is sometimes difficult to discern between roads, driveways, and trails, but, face it, it takes some work to get lost on an island. And then there's the issue of right-of-way. Certain residents are pickier about people crossing their property than others. Some paths are marked with no-trespassing signs, notices beginning "please respect our privacy" or as one sign, posted on a board suspended between stacked milk crates, bluntly states: "No." But there are no chain-link fences and no gated drives. The island is utterly open.

If you desire human contact, your best bet is at the harbor, which might be considered downtown Matinicus. Here you'll find the Pirates Galley restaurant and general store—a good place to catch the latest island news and gossip and to watch the comings and goings in the harbor—the Fisherman's Wife gallery, the town wharf, and the post office. You might even have to wait to use one of the island's "pay" phones— an ordinary phone booth, with a beige plastic wall phone mounted inside—but it's not likely.

The harbor, which is dotted with lobsterboats and is closed in by a large slab granite breakwater, is surrounded by rickety wharves on oily pilings, stacks and stacks of metal lobster traps, and fishing shacks and shanties. There are no fancy homes and not a pleasure boat in sight. If money has touched Matinicus, it's not here.

Heading north from the harbor, past a stand of discarded fuel tanks, the road rises and falls, twists and bends, snaking you toward Markey Beach. The trees once again thicken, and the scents—sun-warmed bayberry, beach rose, blueberry, dust, and fir—are redolent. And then, suddenly, the road opens onto a crescent beach. But this is not just any beach. With its cool breeze, brilliant sun, fine sand, and turquoise water, it feels more Mediterranean than Maine. If this spot were on the mainland, you wouldn't even be able to see the sand for all the bodies. Not so here. You might have to share space with a wading toddler, the occasional sunbather, or a stick-toting black Lab. Maybe.

The same goes for the rest of the island. The south end of the main road passes a shaded graveyard, with its lichen-covered stones, and a number of modest lobstermen's homes with traps and gear piled in the yards. A young mother who is pushing her child on a swing looks up and smiles. A couple stoops to pluck and collect in plastic bags the yellow blooms of Saint Johnswort that grow along the road. Another black Lab (clearly the Matinicus dog of choice) galumphs from his yard to greet you with a tail-wagging frenzy. But these encounters are brief and rare on this road that seems to open up and close in, like some living thing. One minute you are standing before a vast field of swaying goldenrod; the next, you're hemmed in by the dark clutches of gnarled and ancient apple trees gone wild. One turn might lead you down a path where the Queen Anne's lace towers more than six feet tall; another will wend you through the soft cushion of duff and moss on an inland trail; another will take you through the high grass lane that hugs the island's southern wind-swept point; another will land you on South Sandy Beach, a huge scooped-out J of oceanfront. There, you might encounter tots collecting sand dollars and teens rolling driftwood logs down into the water (some odd island game?). All it takes, however, is a quick scramble over the rocks to find yourself alone again with nothing but more island to cover.

Of course, none of this begins to unravel the mystery that is Matinicus. It would be high conceit to think a visit—particularly a casual one—could tell you anything about a culture that is centuries-old. But you are likely to come away knowing something about what August on the coast of Maine used to be like before summer became a marketable commodity.

And, besides, as you wander out to stand beneath a canopy of stars and a sliver of moon that casts more light than many a mainland full moon, you may have but one thought: Some things are better left unexplained.

[2001]

Maine's Best Baguette

You've seen them all over Maine: those signs posted at the end of dirt roads advertising some product—crab meat, corn, firewood, pies, cranberries—for sale from someone's back door. Many of these signs are modest and unpromising. The word "eggs," for example, might be painted in drippy scrawl on a shake shingle or old board. Maybe the neighbor down the road is more enterprising and has added a "farm fresh" in front of her "eggs" and used a neater script. Still, some hesitancy arises. How far down the road? How fresh the eggs or crab? Will a snarling dog leap out at you from under a porch? Will the proprietor be able to make change? Is the sign a ruse? Will you be sported away through some trap door, never to be seen again? (Okay, some of us have more active imaginations than others.) You just never know.

It is thus arresting to come upon a certain sign posted on Route 1 at the head of Ox Cove Road in the wee town of Pembroke. No shake-shingle number, this. It is a professionally painted, tidy white sign with attractive green lettering, befitting the toniest business in a crowded resort area. The thing is, Pembroke is located way Down East in Washington County, where the economy is, at best, shaky and where the tourist industry does not exactly boom. Plus, this forlorn stretch of Route 1, which curves around the western boundary of fingery

Cobscook Bay, can make even the most intrepid Maine traveler feel desolate. You might pass a gas station or package store, but the area does not exactly ring with the bustle of commerce.

It is not, however, the tidiness of the sign that makes it seem so out of place. It's the words it boasts: "Cinqueterre Farm: Organically grown produce. Country bread. Select wine." Cinqueterre? Select wine? *Here*? How? Throwing risk to the wind, you just need to go have a look.

Bumping the mile down Ox Cove Road, you feel yourself to be a New World explorer, a wine-seeking Magellan, a bread-winning Cortés. If there is something to discover at Cinqueterre, surely you will be the first. Or at least that's what you'd like to think.

Pulling into the drive gives nothing away. To your right, a blue, nineteenth-century farmhouse stands on a gently sloping knoll. To your left, a giant pasture is ablaze with wildflowers. In the distance, a sprawling horse barn is sited next to another long, low barn, both of which are painted blue. This could be any farm. For a moment, visions of elderberry wine and dented pans of spongy bread flash across your mind. You tell yourself it's not too late to turn around, but you forge on.

And the moment you pull into the parking area (much to your relief, alongside a couple of other cars) and slide open the door to the shop, you're glad you did. What first hits you is the aroma of freshly baked bread. It's as though you have just walked into an all-engulfing, yeasty, warm cloud. Baking bread is, perhaps, one of the most comforting smells on earth, but this is more than heady, it is heaven. You reel like a drunkard and must steady yourself.

What you first home in on are the baking pans lined with loaves that are stacked on rolling shelving units and the large ovens from which they came. "Bread!" you want to cry. "Give me bread!" But you control yourself. After all, there are others around. You are clearly not the first (or last) to discover Cinqueterre Farm.

As you wait your turn, you survey the rest of the shop, which is housed in a glassed-in patio, framed, you later learn, from lumber harvested and milled on the farm. Through the wide windows, the sun spills in and dazzles the display cases, where bags of homemade granola and jars of preserves and jellies are arranged. A chalkboard lists the items available for specialty orders: pies, brick-oven pizza, cookies, cabbage rolls, baked beans, muffins, croissants. And then there's the honey (120 pounds produced at Cinqueterre in 2001) and the impressive wine and port selection. For anyone who has ever tried to purchase a decent bottle of wine in this corner of the state and been confronted with screw-tops and boxes, Cinqueterre is nothing short of an oasis. Every label has been thoughtfully selected, is reasonably priced (between ten and fifteen dollars), and would satisfy even the biggest wine snob in a pinch.

Gradually, you come to your senses, the transaction before yours is completed, and Gloria Prickett, an ebullient woman in her fifties, with a hank of her thick blond hair pulled up into a ponytail on top of her head, turns her wide smile and attention to you. And, with the same loving care that goes into this little shop—she's all yours.

The mystery and miracle that is Cinqueterre Farm deepens with explanation, and Gloria is happy to share the story and show anyone around who is interested. The enterprise is the brainchild of Gloria, a Maine native, and her husband, Les Prickett, an elegant older man—in a Spencer Tracy-ish sort of way—who moved to the area to "retire" in the 1990s. (Les prefers not to disclose his actual age, but that he served in World War II might give you a clue that retirement could've easily come many years prior.) When not manning the baking ovens in his crisp, heavily starched chef's coat, he can often be found tending to his six hundred acres, caring for his trees, or tilling the garden. "We have his-and-hers tractors," says Gloria with an almost coquettish smile, as she gazes out the window at her husband of just three years.

It's a romance sweetened, perhaps, by a shared love of food. Les is a lifelong and accomplished chef. "I was born to be a cook," he later says. "I knew from the age of twelve that's what I would do."

He began cooking right out of high school, until he was inducted into the service, where he went to cooking school and oversaw the feeding of 350 men. As the officer in charge of supplies, he would often barter with the French locals with surplus items. Grub was no grubby affair under his aegis. He recalls roasting a 350-pound wild boar for his men and supplying them with a bottle of wine each at the table. After the service, he continued in the business and, in 1955, bought the restaurant on the Jersey Shore he would own—despite two failed attempts at retirement—for forty years. He was classically trained at the world-famous Cordon Bleu cooking school in Paris in the 1960s at the same time as Julia Child, although he modestly states they didn't know each other ("We may have brushed arms in the halls") and that he didn't finish, because his money ran out.

The couple first met when Les showed up at Christie's, a restaurant and B&B Gloria—also a lifelong cook—owned for four years in nearby Lubec, because friends had raved about her cooking. When he arrived, however, Gloria informed him the dining room was not open and turned him away, she recalls with a sly grin. Instead, shortly thereafter, she was sitting down to a gourmet meal Les had prepared for her (she can remember every course and every detail) at his home. It was the first of many happy culinary adventures together.

Gloria says she knew the match was going to take when Les transplanted her one thousand raspberry bushes to Cinqueterre from her former home in Lubec. She also notes that in the fall, she climbs into the front-end loader of Les's tractor, so he can raise her up into the limbs of the farm's ancient apple trees to gather fruit for her renowned crab-apple jelly. Call it the Maine version of being swept off your feet.

Of course, the first question is: "Why the name Cinqueterre?" The answer is simple. The land (terre) was acquired in five (cinque) parcels, starting in 1974, when Les purchased the initial piece with his first wife, Betty, after vacationing in the area. Plus, Les had visited the Cinqueterre region of Italy and took a liking to it. "The name just seemed to fit more than Windy Acres or Spruce Point Farm," says Gloria.

Since that time, the farm has been a work in progress. The house is kitchen-centric, with three places to cook at last count, not including the patio baking area. Entering the house from the shop, one first encounters what the couple calls the woodshed or breakfast kitchen, where a turn-of-the-century Round Oak Chief cookstove dominates the room. The ceiling is lined with dark, massive beams, which were salvaged from a barn purchased by Les for said purpose. The other kitchen, called the wood stove or winter kitchen, features cedar cabinets, again made from lumber harvested and milled on the farm by Les. (Prior to the shop, Les had run a sawmill on the property, as well as raised horses.)

But it is the third—the *ecave du vin* kitchen—that astounds. Located in the cellar (not original to the house; Les hired a contractor to dig until he hit ledge), lined with French tile and decorated with leaded glass made by a local glass worker, this remarkable room is more befitting an Italian villa than a Maine farmhouse. Copper pots and cast-iron skillets hang from the ceiling. A huge pastry table fills one corner, while the dining area dominates the opposite one. A huge walk-in fireplace stands at the head of a long harvest table. A throne-like chair, Les's, is placed at the other end. The evening meal—whether it comes from the bean pot or the sauté pan—is an event at Cinqueterre. "We always dress for dinner," says Gloria.

While Gloria is responsible for all the preserving and specialty items, Les is the magic hand behind the bread. To him, the hallmark of cooking is the baguette—a small, narrow loaf of French bread—whose ingredients consist of but four things: organic flour, yeast, salt, and spring water. "[They] don't recognize you as a baker until you make a good baguette," he says firmly. "You have to have the love for it. If your heart isn't in it, the bread is not going to come out."

And to sink your teeth into Les's baguette's crispy crust that yields to the bread's airy, chewy center, you can almost taste the heart and love. Understand, this bread is not good just because of the unlikeliness of finding it here. It could stand up to, and, quite likely surpass, any of the artisan breads being baked in the state—and perhaps anywhere.

Which leads to the inevitable question: How does this business survive in such a remote location? Cinqueterre does just fine. The shop is only open seasonally and, during those months, the Pricketts have a dedicated following, from all walks of life, who line up for the French country, the multi-grain, the raisin, the semolina, the foccacia, or oat loaves, along with all the other offerings. Les's bread is so popular that locals panic if they learn the couple will be away. In fact, Les was supposed to supply bread for a recent, out-of-state family wedding, but had his stocks wiped out by his regular customers before he left and had to stop, en route, at a Portland bakery to buy bread. "It's the classic case of the shoemaker's children," laughs Gloria.

And as you do your part to help deplete the Cinqueterre stocks, leaving laden with assorted jars and loaves (one of which almost doesn't last till the end of the road), you are a little more than pleased with your discovery, despite the fact it's not yours alone. From that moment, you decide you will never look at those dirt-road signs the same way again. Because you just never know.

[2002]

We, Too, Took to the Woods

I cannot say when I first hear the river, exactly. All I know is that one moment the sound is not there, and the next moment it is—faint, but a presence, like distant applause.

We are walking the Carry Road, Husband and I, from where the truck with our gear dumped us off a couple hundred yards back. We'd been bumping over gated logging roads for half an hour or better, first in our car, then, when the road got too rough, in the back of the truck. But I wanted to take this last leg by foot. I did not want to rush my first glimpse of the place that is so familiar, yet I have never seen.

Suddenly, I spot it, poking up through the canopy of trees that line the road: the peak of a roof. As we crest a small grade to a clearing, the whole house opens into full view: a one-story cabin, painted spearmint green with forest-green trim and with a porch fronting both the road and the river. I'd like to say this is the "Aha!" moment I'd been waiting for, but the only photographs I have seen of this, the Winter House, were taken with snow piled to the windows. But then I turn and look up the river, and a breathless elation shakes me. There, stretching across the gentle rips like a saggy covered bridge to nowhere, is Pondy Dam—just like the photograph in the book. Even though we have only arrived, I know at this moment I will be able to hereafter claim: We took to the woods.

I am referring, of course, to that beloved Maine classic by Louise Dickinson Rich, which, when published in 1942, became an instant bestseller, putting this far-flung five miles or so of dirt road and river, located between the Rangeley Lakes Region of Maine and the New Hampshire border, on the national map. And I am here, by special arrangement with the current owner, on a literary pilgrimage of sorts. I have come to stay in Rich's actual house for a long summer weekend and to find the world and the life she so vividly described.

Even though for years I had seen copies of *We Took To The Woods* shelved in used bookstores, I wasn't compelled to read it until my honeymoon, which was spent in a borrowed eighteenth-century Cape in Down East Machiasport (yes, by choice!) in 1999. It rained almost all that week, and Husband and I spent a good deal of time not far from the kitchen's huge cookstove that heated the house, sniffling (we had both come down with colds) and reading. The minute I turned to the opening paragraph of Rich's book, I knew I had found a kindred spirit:

"[W]hen asked [during adolescence] what I was going to do with my life," she wrote, "[I said] that I was going to live alone in a cabin in the Maine woods and write." Me, too! Further, she was mildly astonished to find that "grown to womanhood, I seem to be living in a cabin in the Maine woods, and I seem to be writing." Me, too! (Except my "cabin" turned out to be an office overlooking Portland's Congress Street.) Louise and I had also foregone the "alone" part; we were both newly married (I later in life than she; but her 1930s world made her seem older than her years).

As I read on, I discovered neither of us cared much for the culinary arts. (She, however, did not have the good sense to marry an able and willing cook, so she spent much of her day at the stove.) We both liked being one of the boys. (She went to elaborate lengths to brag how she was a better hand on a two-man cross-cut saw than a lot of professional woodsmen, which sounds like something I would do). Neither she nor I were primpers. As she said: "I can't stand having things tight around my waist or neck or wrists [me, either!], and you can't be stylish unless you have your clothes anchored in a few places, at least." Neither of us liked to be jostled or have anyone crowd us, either literally or figuratively. And we were both rather—how, gentle reader, shall I put this?—flip. ("I like a dash of irony in my dish," she quipped.) But when I read the words: "Writing is not all beer and skittles," that sealed the deal. I knew I liked Louise. A lot.

We Took To The Woods is something of a Q&A–type conversation with the reader. Each chapter poses a question—"Don't You Ever Get Bored?" "Aren't You Ever Frightened?" "Isn't Housekeeping Difficult?"—about Louise's strange life of self-imposed hardship and exile at Forest Lodge with her husband, Ralph; their little boy, Rufus; the handyman, Gerrish; and the rotating cast of characters —the woodsmen, the "sports" (tourists), the neighbors—who filter through their lives and people her lively 1930s woods tableau.

Her "responses" are largely anecdotal, often nesting more questions and answers inside the greater ones, and they are stuffed with detail WTTTW devotees can list off the oddball and exotic place names—Middle Dam ("Middle"), Lakewood Camps ("Coburn's"), South Arm ("the Arm"), Sunday Cove ("the Cove"), Sunday Pond, B Pond (and the "despised B Pond trail"), Brown Farm (not a farm), Umbagog Lake (pronounced um-BAY-gog), the towns of Magalloway, Upton, and Andover and, of course, Pond-in-the-River ("Pondy"), Pondy Dam, the Carry Road, the Rapid River. And then there is Forest Lodge itself, which is made up of the rambling Summer House (their main residence), the Winter House (not much more than a one-room cabin, but the only structure they could adequately heat in the coldest months), and numerous outbuildings. True aficionados can as quickly cite their favorite passages: Louise's do-it-yourself homebirth of Rufus ("I told [Ralph] where to find the blanket, in between pains, and he went away again. When he came back, five minutes later, he was a father."); the pet skunk, Rollo; the sneakers and wool socks Louise wore all winter in lieu of boots; her first trip to the Outside in four years. ("In," "Out" and the "Outside" are always capped in the book; trips to the Outside were mandatory lest one got "woods queer"—getting upset over breaking one's "pet needle," for example.)

Although Rich, who died in 1991 at the age of eighty-eight, authored more than twenty books, none quite so strongly resonates as *We Took To The Woods*. This is, perhaps, because of her wonderment, the awe and delight contained in her responses. It's as though she can't quite believe she's made a life for herself and her family out in the distant outpost (yes, by choice!) any more than we can. And it is the candor and humor—that conversational feel—that have made so many readers regard her as a friend. And I'm just about to track down that friend and that life I feel I know so well.

I tentatively approach the Winter House, where Husband and I will be staying. I've made numerous literary pilgrimages before to roped-off rooms artfully pieced back together to recreate a writer's life—a pair of reading glasses here, an opened text there—and they usually disappoint. At such places, one does not touch, one does not engage, one does not enter in. One views, and from a distance.

But here I am, stomping across Louise's porch, lugging a handle of Poland Spring water (no, it's not the same as carting a bucket up from the river like she had to, but it's the best I can do), swinging open her door and letting it bang shut behind me, just as she probably did countless times. Even though it is high noon in the thick of summer, the interior is steeped in the "sunless gloom" the book describes, and it takes my eyes more than a couple of minutes to adjust. But, slowly, things take shape: the fireplace that juts out four feet into the long, narrow, and already cramped room (Husband instantly declares he'd last about a winter weekend in such close quarters) and the adjacent woodstove; the "wallpaper"—cartoons and advertisements from period magazines pasted to the walls—and the hand-rubbed pine paneling. I can see how the sunny bedrooms overlook the river, while the living room faces the dark woods and road (so one could keep tabs on passers-by, according to Louise)—an arrangement that irritated her, and as I grope around, I concur. But Louise and I are not complainers. We make do.

I instantly set about my homely duties—making the bed, putting away clothes, and stocking our larder (in the book, there was no kitchen in the Winter House; food was ferried over in all weather from the Summer House kitchen) with the overwhelming amount of supplies we've packed in for our three days. I mean, really, really overwhelming. That's because my most memorable passages from *WTTTW* concern food: Louise's utterly icky sounding "desperation dishes," such as Mock Tripe made from oatmeal-pot leavings or her Vienna sausage, baked beans, and ketchup casserole; how she stretched provisions (peeling potatoes paper thin and diluting canned milk with too much water); feeding lost hunters and stray woodsmen on nearly nothing (as she said, it wasn't like you could send them down the road to the hot-dog cart); and the importance of The List. Supplies came in once a week in summer and once a month (at best) in winter. Meals depended on "how bright or dull" she and Ralph were while making out the list and on their finances, which were, more often than not, grim. "Once a thing is forgotten," she wrote, "it's forgotten until next time."

Well, I don't take want as well as Louise did. And a next time, for us, was unlikely. So I started our list a week before the trip and left it out on the dining room table for Husband's additions, since he would be doing the cooking. (All my dishes start or end in desperation for everyone concerned; I know to give the skillet a wide berth.) The shopping itself was saved for the day before departure. Suddenly, food items that had, up until that point in my life, held no interest—ugly fruit, pimento loaf, Count Chocula cereal—took on grave import. Could I live without tofu meatballs for three days? I wondered, pondering the vacuum-sealed package in my grip. It was a very slow shop.

Packing was worse. I will spare you the details, but let it be said that when all our bags and coolers had been off-loaded from the truck onto the Winter House porch, there was no doubt about it: We were sports.

Be that as it may, sports—kayakers, white-water rafters, Outward Bounders, and, especially, anglers—are a large part of the population (and economy) these days on the Rapid River and at Forest Lodge, which has for years been used as a classic Maine sports camp. As remote as we are, there is a constant flotilla of various watercraft on the river and parade of portagers and anglers along the Carry Road. Forest Lodge is owned by Aldro French, whose father bought the property in 1966, and who has been a presence here ever since.

And quite a presence he is. As we wander next door to the Summer House—a rambling structure, built into the side of granite ledge, hovering over the river (again, just like the picture)—French tears up on an ATV, fresh from a rafting trip with some of his guests. A big bear of a man with a barrel chest, a shock of white hair, and a bushy white mustache, and who punctuates the ends of his sentences with a resounding "yessah," French prefers to be referred to as keeper of the lodge, rather than its owner. And he has done justice to his title. Although most of the sports who come to stay at Forest Lodge and fish the famed Rapid River with French as their guide have no idea about the Rich legacy, he has reverently kept the compound as close to historically intact as is possible without putting up velvet ropes. The occasional library or educational group that comes "in" for tours (by special arrangement with French) is not disappointed. There's a thrill of recognition at every turn.

We start in the spacious living room, and French points out artifacts: Louise's rocker, her roll-top desk (both purchased with "success money" from *WTTTW*, he tells me), the upright piano with the harpsichord twang that Ralph played, Louise's typewriter placed on a metal stand. He shows me her writing nook, located in a cramped corner of this great room in front of a tall window, and the shelves of books—dusty, cloth-bound volumes that would look at home in any old Maine camp—she left behind, along with all these other things.

(The post-*WTTTW*, real-life Louise Dickinson Rich story is not a particularly happy one. Ralph died only two years after the book's publication. Louise fled, only to return for a time and produce two more books about her life in this area [whose pages, by comparison, do not turn so lightly as those of *WTTTW*] before heading "out" for good. When she left Forest Lodge, her exodus was swift and, according to

French, she never returned, which explains why so many of her possessions remain.)

Upstairs, the small bedrooms where anglers sleep are spartan affairs—bare wood walls and floors, but with eagle-eye views of the river. I would like to say I can imagine Rufus being born up here on that frigid December night, with no one attending but Ralph, but I cannot. While I feel I share a kinship with Louise, this is an area in which we part ways. In fact, I hold close—maybe even cling a little—to the hand-smoothed newel post as we return downstairs. I can be a tad clumsy, and the birth/bedroom reminds me how far we are from the nearest nice, sterile, shiny E.R.

Rich family photographs are framed and mounted around the house. Volumes of her books are set out on tables. French produces a neat stack of Louise's canceled checks (smalls sums for all the usual mundane domestic necessities), the tidy fountain pen script faded to a watery blue. He shows me a fan letter, which is fragile with age in my hands, and I am happy when he restores it to safekeeping.

And that's the miracle of today's Forest Lodge—how all this history is lived with. The rooms in the Summer House are used as common areas, in which any guest of the lodge is free to roam. Louise's rocker is pulled in among the ring of chairs surrounding the huge stone fireplace, which you know sees heavy action after a long day of chasing trout. The desk is bursting with French's personal papers. Decades-old magazines are stacked on every available surface, as though they have just arrived and are waiting to be read. "Go ahead, sit in her chair," French encourages, gesturing with his large hand. I alight gently, give a couple rocks and spring back out. (I guess I should've experienced some sort of writerly connection to Louise, but I didn't.) Nor do I feel compelled to test out her writing nook or rest my fingertips on the keys of her typewriter. I'm content to view, and from a distance.

I go stand on the porch and listen for a moment to the relentless roar of the river, which drops 185 feet in three miles with no falls, and I think of Louise's words when asked if the sound of the river got on her nerves: "You learn to pitch your voice, not louder to carry over it, but lower and deeper, so that it's not shattered by the vibration." I try it, and she's right.

Much, in fact, is right, but there's still something missing, although I can't say just what. All the physical things measure up. The Summer House continues to be balanced on poles. Ralph's shop matches the book's rendering, right down to his workbench, complete with narrow drawers holding rusted screws and hardware. Gerrish's shack is now a fly shop, but retains its rustic feel. The Carry Road is little changed. While Forest Lodge is no longer the "sole address" here, only two additional private camps have been built since *WTTTW*, thanks to French's preservation efforts and the Rapid River Conservation Easement.

A hike down to Louise's picnic spot at Smooth Ledge and her swimming hole at Long Pool prove they are as she described them sixty years ago. The paddle Husband and I later take via Pond-in-the-River up to Middle Dam offers the same vista of hills pictured in the book. Ghosts hover, too: traces of Louise's vegetable garden on the knoll in front of the Winter House; the rusted husk of the 1924 Marmon (one of their workhorse cars), which is beached in the woods behind the Summer House; and, tucked amid the trees on the shore at Pondy, the skeletal remains—two curled, sled-like runners; a tall, crooked chimney pot; and a base—of the winch boat *Alligator*, a sort of barge used for booming (or herding up) logs. And (in case you're wondering) trips to the privy behind Gerrish's shop are still the "character building" experience Louise claimed them to be. In fact, it's clear that most every action here—from making a shopping list to clearing the Carry Road of snow—required character-building effort. This was no easy life.

So, yes, all of these things are right, but I still haven't found Louise. And what better place to look, I decide, than on a walk up to Lakewood Camps at Middle Dam. I know the distance to Middle is only two miles, and I know the phone line for the crank phones (still in service to keep people along the Carry Road connected—there is no phone service to the Outside; even cell phones have no reception along the river), which is slung from tree to tree or on the ground, will guide me. But I'm not taking any chances. As Louise said: "[T]here is nothing to be afraid of in the woods, except yourself. If you've got sense, you can keep out of trouble. If you haven't got sense, you'll get into trouble, here or anywhere else."

Even she, however, didn't always follow her own advice and managed to get lost in her own backyard—on a trek over to B Pond undertook just to prove her guiding ability ("the least worthy excuse for taking a chance," she said). While I would like to follow in her footsteps as much as possible, I won't if it means they are going to leave me stranded out in the woods and late for dinner. Because Husband is at this moment nothing more than a fly-casting dot in the middle of the river up at Pondy Dam, I prepare. I equip myself with water, a compass, a map, a walkie-talkie, plus I leave a note stating my destination, my departure time, my estimated time of return and the companion walkie-talkie. And, since I don't own a wristwatch, I fold up my travel alarm clock, slip it in my pocket and set off clinking and clanking down the road, muttering "sport."

Poised as I am for some ill to befall me, I make it to Lakewood Camps and back safely—with numerous woods detours—before anyone even notices I'm gone. I kick off my boots, open a beer (first item on The List), and settle into one of the Adirondack chairs perched on the point, overlooking Pondy Dam, and feel momentarily—as Louise would say—"bum."

But toward the end of our visit, it dawns on me what is missing: This trip has been Louise Lite. The beauty of *We Took To The Woods* is the adventure and mishap, the hardship and making-do—and, more than anything else, weather. Our visit has been an idyll. Nothing crucial was forgotten. The days have been spectacular—no hurricanes, no twenty-below mornings, no blizzards, or driving rain. What I have found here is a movie set—a true-to-life backdrop, replete with authentic props—but that's all. And that, perhaps, is the problem with this (and any) pilgrimage: There is no livelier or lovelier Forest Lodge than the one that exists in my imagination from reading the book. Even as I sit in the thick of the real *We Took To The Woods,* when I close my eyes, I still see *my* version, and my version looks like old-timey log-drive footage—brownish and scratchy—and not much like this beautiful place I've been poking around for the past couple of days. Well, then. That's the reason I couldn't find Louise: She's been with me all along, right upstairs, in my old noggin.

Am I disappointed? Not at all. Because I have to come up with the same answer Louise did when she asks herself in the final chapter of the book, "Is It Worth-while?":

It's enough that it was fun.

[2003]

Black Mountain Bear

It's not surprising the conversation turns—as it often does when one is in the Maine woods—to bears. My husband and I are folded into the jump seats of Beth and Jim's pickup truck, rattling down a dirt road to the trailhead of Black Mountain, one peak over from Schoodic in Hancock County.

Beth, who was raised in nearby Sorrento, was my college roommate for two of my three semesters at Orono in the late 1970s. We've managed to remain close, even though she left the state right after school to work on and captain boats up and down the eastern seaboard, and beyond. She and her husband, Jim—a Minnesota farm boy turned yacht captain—return only sporadically to the home they built on family land in Sorrento via fax and phone from the Caribbean. This most recent Maine stint, despite frequent trips and travel, has been relatively long—a couple of years. But now, they are preparing to head out to launch a client's brand-new, 126-foot power yacht (the construction of which Jim commuted to Wisconsin to oversee) into Lake Michigan. They'll eventually make the voyage up the St. Lawrence, into the Atlantic, and to ports unknown, and it's not certain when we'll see each other again. So, this is something of a farewell hike—a proper Maine sendoff to our seafaring friends.

Although each of us has put in our share of woods time, no one has actually seen a bear. This opens the floor for near-miss stories, and my husband dusts off his greatest hit, which opens with his waking to the sound of a bear snurfing around outside his tent and closes with a hysterical woman a couple of campsites over, shrieking in a nasally New York accent, "Oh my gawd, he's got the banana bread."

We then, of course, move on to the topic of: What to Do If You See a Bear. As I said, none of us are strangers to the outdoors, but the variety of theories we come up with is truly remarkable: climb a tree, don't climb a tree, drop and play dead, give it a look like it has a bad haircut and slowly back off, and my personal contribution, whack it on the nose. Everyone laughs, but I stand firm. What I don't tell them is most of my bear ken was derived from the opening chapters of Bill Bryson's book about hiking the Appalachian Trail, *A Walk in the Woods,* in which he vividly describes every which way a human can meet with an untimely end at the maw and paw of a bear. I don't recall many of the specifics—Bryson had taken most of his information from a book entitled, *Bear Attacks: Their Causes and Avoidance,* and there were way too many dos and don'ts to keep track of—but the basic gist I took away was that a bear attack in the eastern U.S. is unlikely, and if you happen to fall prey to one, good luck to you.

We discuss flight or fight, and everyone seems to think hanging around to duke it out with an attacking bear is not all that appealing, when running like a maniac is an option. (As Bryson says, "[running] will give you something to do with the last seven seconds of your life.") We all agree noise is a yes, since bears don't like to be taken by surprise, but that begs the question, what kind of noise? (Almost every bear book includes the joke: How do you tell grizzly scat from black bear scat? The grizzly scat has the bear bells in it.) Frankly, I don't much care for being taken by surprise, either—especially by a creature that with one swipe can remove my face—and, to my mind, announcing my presence with clanging and bell-ringing and singing is not only uncomely, but it seems to be asking for trouble.

We take the easy, half-mile walk in from the parking area to the trailhead at Donnell Pond, where, despite the gray chill of late April, a group of hippie kids has set up a tent-world compound at the primitive campsite. Smoke rises from a fire pit and clothing is slung over makeshift clotheslines. Two young women, their hair wrapped in bandanas, pad around the site and give us a blasé wave as we pass.

It takes a little doing to locate the trail from the beach, but since most of the trees have only started to bud, we eventually find a few with blue slash marks on them and head in. As with many hikes, the initial assent is swift, and we all try to hide our huffing from each other. When one of us stops for a breather, we all happily join in.

As we progress, we fall into our hiking rhythm. We pair up for conversations—How are the last stages of the ship construction coming? Do you think you'll drive or fly out? Should we try to arrange one more visit before you go?—but after a time, we stake out our own part of the trail and are alone with our thoughts.

And that's when I spot it.

At first, "it" is nothing more than a dark hulking lump out of the corner of my eye. When I turn to look, my mind says, "Ha, ha—a bear. We were talking about bears, and now you think you see one," in the same way that if you stare at an object and then close your eyes, you see it on the back of your lids. But this bear is not on the back of my eyelids. It is right over there, pawing at the soft earth, just off the trail—maybe fifty yards away. I am in the lead, but we are all fairly close together. I slowly turn on my heel and silently mouth as wide as I can the word "BEAR." Everyone instantly spots it and freezes. We have, at last, been put to the test: What do we do now?

I would like to report there is a definitive answer, but in all the subsequent reading and asking around I do after our encounter, what I find out can best be encapsulated by the not wholly comforting opening line of *Backcountry Bear Basics: The Definitive Guide to Avoiding Unpleasant Encounters,* by Dave Smith, which reads: "Bear literature is confusing and contradictory."

Elizabeth Peavey

A few things, however, seem generally agreed upon. You need to know if you're dealing with a black bear or a grizzly, because they are not the same species and react differently. (The grizzly is more ferocious.) The bad news is that it's not always easy to tell them apart. Even bear experts can have trouble, Smith tells us. The good news is there are no grizzlies east of the Mississippi. There are, however, somewhere between 500,000 and 700,000 black bears in North America, and Maine is said to have one of the highest concentrations, with around 22,000 to 23,000. The male black bear weighs in anywhere between 250 and 600 pounds (quite a discrepancy, if you ask me); the female, a daintier 100 to 400 pounds. The only mention I find concerning how to differentiate between the sexes involves the direction of the urine stream (the female jets backwards; the male straight down), but I want to be in no position to make that inquiry or discovery.

Another accepted fact is that black bears are omnivores and are almost never sated. Smith asserts bears are finicky, even though they're willing to give anything (including a laptop computer) a taste-test. Author Ben East (born in 1898) takes a less gracious view in his 1977 book, *Bears: A Veteran Outdoorsman's Account of the Most Fascinating and Dangerous Animals in North America,* where he quotes an old timer as saying: "A bear will eat anything a hog will eat, and some things a hog won't look at." He also says that bear attacks, both provoked and unprovoked, "occur too often to be counted," but the book is primarily about hunting, so his side of the issue may be a tad shaded.

But the big question remains: What should one do when confronted with bears or the possibility thereof? Well, everyone concurs the first and most important thing is not to be stupid with food in the woods. Put the banana bread away. Don't leave garbage around. And never feed bears. "A fed bear's a dead bear," says Smith. Once they've tasted human food, there's no turning back. Also, it is agreed you should never run from a bear. Not only will it sound the dinner bell in their brains, but black bears clock around twnety-five or thirty miles per hour. If you want to believe the old myth that they can't run well downhill, that's up to you. (See you in the ICU.) Tree climbing is a no for black bears, although it's a yes for grizzlies. (If you have trouble remembering, try this little rhyme I just made up: "Grizz-a-lee, climb a tree. Big black bear, don't you dare.") You're also not supposed to look a bear in the eye, since it's taken as an affront, and the last thing you want to do is offend a bear.

So you don't run. You don't climb a tree. You don't ogle. What do you do? Well, that's where the confusing and contradictory part comes in. Almost all sources say if it's a black bear, do not drop and play dead. (That's what you do for a grizzly attack.) Although, in their 1991 book, *The Appalachian Trail Backpacker,* Victoria and Frank Logue, referencing the National Park Service, say to assume the fetal position on the ground; that most bears will leave you alone or "content themselves with a scratch or two." One wonders, though, if there have been any recent titles from this couple, who might want to read some of the books I have.

In the end, the best I can deduce from my research is this: Stand your ground. Even backing away can prompt a predatory or even curious bear to want to investigate. If the bear approaches, make noise. Big noise. The Maine Department of Inland Fisheries and Wildlife Web site even suggests yelling and rushing toward the bear, which I would do only if someone from that agency lead the charge *and* I were in a Humvee. If the bear charges, continue to hold your ground—up until about fifteen feet. Then, if you happen to be prescient enough to have pepper spray with you, you may employ it at this time. Otherwise, it's up to you to fight for your life. I feel vindicated to find one source on the Internet—the Maine Resource Guide Network—that says "[M]any lives have been saved by striking the bear on the nose," although they may have acquired their information from the Logues' book. It is also widely suggested you find a weapon of some sort and avoid using your bare hands for battle, since it wouldn't take much effort for a bear to dis-arm you.

The best bit of news, however, is that most experts say you can usually simply shoo black bears away. Plus, according to Smith, black bears, when threatened, retreat. But please don't take my word for any of this. I'm just reporting all the contradictory information I found. Besides, there might be one grizzly out there who's hopped a train back East or a lone black bear who isn't up on his behavior code, and I don't want to bear the responsibility for anyone's encounters.

So, speaking of encounters, how do we four fare? Pretty well, it turns out, but not by design. No one in our party heads for a tree or drops and plays dead. What we do is gawk. As the bear continues to ignore us, we grow more brazen. We lift our binoculars. He's a beauty. His deep, thick fur is without a hint of post-hibernation mange or bed head. We exchange remarks. Beth takes a couple pictures, even though we know they'll be little more than dark splotches. Every so often, a thought brushes across my mind: "Why do I feel so calm? Should we be doing something? Are we in danger?" But what really holds us all in place in sheer awe.

Suddenly the bear looks up at us. "Come on, brain," I say. "Give me a little direction here." But I get nothing. Apparently none of us do. We just stand and watch as this great beast turns with the greatest speed and agility, and thunders off into the woods.

For the longest time, we don't move or speak. We may be thinking we've just had a close call. Or that we really need to bone up on our bear facts. Or that we've just had an extraordinary experience. One way or the other, though, we have been given a grand gift from the Maine woods.

And what better sendoff is there than that?

[2005]

Taking Mount Kineo

As we snake through Greenville at this early morning hour, en route to Rockwood to catch the launch for Mount Kineo, the town almost looks the way my husband and I are used to seeing Maine: a quarter-to-desolate. We try to avoid the state's hot spots during the in-season, preferring, instead the off- (or better yet) off-off-season. I cannot too highly sing the praises of Carrabassett Valley in July or Stongington in February. Almost any place in the state is safe in March and November; I don't mind that the gewgaw shop is closed or the wraps-n-wings restaurant has shuttered for the season. Seeing the state when others have fled not only makes us feel like lone pioneers, but we also don't have to share.

So when we arrived in the Moosehead Lake area the day before in the lovely arc of an ebbing August afternoon, I shouldn't have been surprised there was but one remaining campsite in Lily Bay State Park. But I was. I knew that while most of the park's nearly one hundred campsites had long been booked, a handful of non-reserved sites are held aside for people like me who prefer spontaneity over the certainty they'll have a place to sleep. I just assumed we would collect one of those sites upon our arrival. It didn't occur to me so many others would beat us to the punch.

As Husband and I stood staring at the campsite's unsatisfactory location on a map at the park's check-in station—okay, "campsite" is a little generous; it was more of a traffic circle—I wanted to stomp my foot and demand the ranger cough up one of the beautiful, isolated, lakeside spots for which the park is famed. "You're not going to plunk us down in the middle of all those . . . *people*?" I almost blurted, but then thought better of it. It was I, after all, who had suggested this high-season driving tour. "Come on," I'd said. "It'll be fun! We can go swimming." Complaining now would not only be pointless, but would also draw attention to the number of wrong calls I was accumulating on this vacation. It was also I who pushed to depart our equally unsatisfactory, high-season campsite in Down East Cobscook Bay State Park much, much earlier in the day for Moosehead—"Come on," I'd said. "It'll be fun!"—a "jaunt" that turned out to be nearly two hundred miles long.

No, my best course of action was to buck up for our two-night minimum, particularly since my dear, patient spouse was being heroically mum on the subject. We would make the most of it, I decided, even as we pulled into our site to find our neighbors gone and their golden retriever, who had been left tied to the picnic table, highly agitated by our every movement. "Arf, arf," he said as our gear came out and our tent went up. "Arf, arf," he said as I changed my shoes. "Arf, arf," he said at each car and camper that rumbled by. "Arf," he said at absolutely nothing at all.

I had to think fast.

I raced back to the ranger station for camp wood and inspiration and spotted a brochure about Mount Kineo. Mount Kineo! Hiking it was something I had long wanted to do, but because I knew it could only be accessed by water, the prospect always seemed like too much trouble and would take too much time. Ah, but time we had. We could make a day of it. Husband was game, and I was temporarily off the hook.

Mount Kineo is easily one of the state's most distinctive landmarks.

Many people think it's sited on an island (until this trip, myself included), which isn't true, but might just as well be, since the 1,150-acre
Kineo Peninsula (800 acres of which was purchased by the state in
1990 with money from the Land for Maine's Future Fund) is not accessible by public road. Surging out of the center of Moosehead Lake, rising to 1,789 feet at its summit and with an eastern cliff face that drops
a heart-thumping 700 feet, Mount Kineo commands your attention. It
is best viewed (aside from on the lake itself) from the public landing on
the western shore at Rockwood. Looking at its great, dark bulk hulking
on the horizon, you understand the mystical quality that has been attributed to it and attracted visitors for centuries.

One legend says that from an ancient tribe the great hunter
Glusquehbeh (sometimes referred to as Gluskabe, sometimes Gluskap)
felled a great bull moose in the lake, leaving his shoulders to bleach in
the sun, and that's how Kineo got its shape. Another legend tells of the
hunter/warrior Kinneho, who left his tribe (after maybe or maybe not
killing his mother) to dwell alone above the mountain's cliffs, returning
but once to help defend his tribe against the Penobscot Indians. When
he died, it is said, the mountain cleaved open and swallowed him up—
all of which, perhaps, saved us from having to spell and say Mount
Glusquehbeh.

For thousands of years, native peoples traveled great distances to
Kineo to gather rhyolite, a volcanic stone highly prized for tool and
weapon making. (This material has oft erroneously been identified as
flint, but there is no flint in Maine.) In the early nineteenth century, the
first lodging house went up, serving as a midpoint stopover for loggers
traveling Moosehead's forty miles. The steamship arrived in 1836, then
the "sports" followed. Thoreau made a noted visit to the area in 1857
and later called Mount Kineo "the celebrated precipice" in his book *The
Maine Woods*. It was during the late nineteenth and early twentieth centuries, however, that Kineo saw its heyday. The flat, southern foot of the
peninsula was home to a series of resorts that burned and were rebuilt,

culminating in the Mount Kineo House, one of the era's largest inland waterfront hotels in America. At full-tilt, the hotel could accommodate seven hundred guests, and grandly, with every imaginable modern convenience of the day. There was also a golf course, one of the earliest built in New England, circa 1880, that is still in operation. Gracious private cottages sprung up along the adjacent shoreline. Kineo was, in a word, an absolute tourist hot spot for the well-heeled Eastern traveler. But, like many resorts of its kind, it began a slow decline in the late 1930s, from which it never recovered. The hotel is gone, long since burned and demolished. And while there have been various lodging and dining establishments there since that time (and a failed attempt at a massive development project in the 1970s), today's Kineo is, by comparison, sleepy. And sleepy is what makes this morning's trek so appealing.

I had made sure we were on the road with gobs of extra time for the 9 A.M. boat, but as we make our way past the not-quite-yet-up-and-at-'em Greenville and north on Route 15, I envision lines already forming at the dock and perhaps a little nasty elbow action taking place for a seat on the launch. I needn't have worried, however. When we arrive (with plenty of time to spare), there's not much activity. The launch—which looks a little like a miniature steamboat, with a single deck covered by a roof—is tied up and empty. Husband and I take a spot on the grassy knoll that borders the parking lot, have a bit of breakfast, and wait. Eventually, another car pulls up, and a middle-age couple unloads golf clubs, which clank and clatter as they make their way down to the dock. This has all the appearance of a queue starting to form, so I dump the remainder of my granola and secure a stubborn seat near the boat. I am not taking any chances.

Again, I needn't have worried. At a moment before nine, the "captain" arrives (a bare-chested, hippie-looking kid, with his mass of corkscrew curls tied up in a scarf), as well as another golfing couple and their nine-year-old daughter carting her wee bag of clubs. Once they join our party, we're off.

The crossing is brief—less than a mile. As Mount Kineo looms ahead, I think we may be in for more hike than we bargained for. (All my guidebooks rated it as "easy.") But we are prepared with good boots, a trail map, water, and, most important, lunch. Plus, we have an entire day to fill.

After we dock, we all make our way up the gravel drive toward the golf course. To our left, the Mount Kineo House's abandoned dormitory—a long, barracks-style building, several stories tall, with the windows smashed out—sits derelict in the middle of a scrubby field. Meanwhile, that Kineo cliff face continues to stare us down. We lose the golfers at the pro shop, keep our eyes peeled for shanked or sliced balls as we scoot across the eighth fairway, and find the start of the Carriage Trail, which hugs the western side of Kineo and also hooks up to the two summit trails. According to my books, the preferred hike is the steep but scenic Indian Trail, four miles, roundtrip, from dock to summit. We, however, choose the Bridle Trail, which is less steep and less dramatic, but covers more ground. Our plan is to take as much of Kineo as we can on this day. And, besides, we've already encountered a number of people on the trail (in addition to the launch, many access the peninsula with private or rental boats), and we're ready to once again be lone pioneers. We enter at the second trailhead and are swallowed into Kineo.

While the deeply forested Bridle Trail is not grueling, it gives the old pipes a workout here and there. We meet up with the Indian Trail about halfway to the summit and at a bald outcropping get our first real vista—a sweeping backward glance at Rockwood. If this were a life-list/Maine-Merit-Badge–type of mission we were on ("Kineo. Check. Done that. Next . . ."), our hike could end here. We've already seen plenty. But this is just the start.

The view at the summit is largely obscured by trees, but there's a fire tower for those who can stomach the climb. Above us, a bespectacled, gangly youth stiffly makes his way down with a death grip on the railing, chanting his new mantra: "I like heights! I like heights!," while his father coaches him on. When his sneakers finally plant on terra firma, he looks ready to drop to his knees and kiss the ground—and he probably would've had we not been there.

Now it's our turn. The metal stairs are extremely narrow, and each step you take seems to ring through you. The paint on the railing is flaking, making a death grip a little awkward for sliding your hand. I concentrate on my feet as I ascend and watch the ground below grow distant. No need to look up until there's something to see, right? Just one foot in front of the other—bong, bong, bong. Finally, I lift my head. There, in 360-degree splendor, is the great expanse of hills and mountains that circle Moosehead Lake. The water below is flat and blue. Rockwood is a dot. Boats are white mites. I can feel the tower's frame gently swaying. (That's good, right? Towers want give, don't they?) The wind is stiff. My eyes tear. But, finally, I can breathe.

Instead of backtracking, we have chosen to return via the North Trail, which, according to our map, will take us down the back side of the mountain and then connect with the Carriage Trail at Hardscrabble Point. From there, it's just a couple of miles back to the dock. Piece of cake.

The North Trail takes a sudden and steep descent from the summit. The trees are so tall and thick, it's dusky. The going is not so fast, but that gives us time to drink up the sweet air that is filled with the scent of . . . what is that? I know that smell. We look down at our ankles. Blueberries! And not just little patches here and there—but blankets of them—blankets of the biggest, roundest, fattest, sweetest blue-black berries I have ever seen or tasted, as though they had sprouted up from the forest primeval. Now we are officially dawdling. These berries cannot be passed by. We pluck at the bushes as we walk, occasionally stopping to collect fistfuls that we shove into our mouths. We gorge like big old bears, until we are all but lumbering down this hill in our splendid solitude. Not once do we encounter another person—not a soul—nor does it look like anyone has used this trail for ages. By the time we

reach Hardscrabble Point, we feel as though we have the whole state to
ourselves.

At the point, there are three state-owned, primitive campsites (vacant, happily), a privy, and a stretch of beach with a cluster of shade
trees. Hanging from one of them is a nice swing that almost demands a
spin. The plank that serves as a seat is wide enough for an adult butt,
so I get out of my boots and sail up into the sky from which it feels we
have just descended. We soak our feet, make lengthy deliberations
about whether or not to have a swim (too chilly, we conclude), have our
lunch, beach comb (and are shocked and delighted to find "lake
glass"—the equivalent of sea glass, which has been tumbled and
smoothed by water and stones). The afternoon ticks away, yet we linger.

Eventually, a powerboat arrives, putters back and forth along what
I now consider to be our beach, and finds a spot at the other end to
land. Two Labs leap out of the boat, circle frantically around, and then
plop down onto the shore. The couple hauls out two lawn chairs, plant
them so they face out toward the lake, and settle in them. When the
boat arrived, the first thing I'd said was "Let's go." But now as I see this
couple and their dogs down at the far end of the beach doing nothing
more than sitting, gazing out at the lake, just like we are, I half hope
they might look up in our direction, so I might wave.

After all, I decide, as I climb aboard for one last swing before we
head back, there's plenty of Kineo to go around.

[2004]

Life in an Outpost

If you had told Shirley Raymond when she was growing up in Rhode Island in the 1950s she would end up as an adult living fifty or sixty miles from the nearest clothing store, hospital, or voting booth, in a place where she would be called upon to suture split lips and set broken limbs, deliver death notices and bushwhack backwoods trails, put up walls and roof buildings, as well as run a store and feed hundreds of people over the course of a winter weekend, she probably would have told you you were nuts.

But, then, who wouldn't?

Yet that is exactly the life Shirley and her husband, Ed Raymond, chose for themselves when they decided to pack in their jobs at Texas Instruments in Attleboro, Massachusetts, and head for a remote outpost in the great North Woods of Maine in the late 1970s. Despite all the challenges—and there have not been few—they've never looked back.

The first question, obviously, is, Why? Why would someone want this life? To find out, you might want to stop by Raymond's Country Store in Northeast Carry, Maine (year-round population: two), for a direct answer. It's a long, bumpy ride from Greenville—almost all of it over logging roads—to the Carry, which is located at the northeasternmost corner of Moosehead Lake. If you are expecting a rustic log cabin tucked in the pines, you'll probably be surprised when you arrive. What the Raymonds have going here can only be called a compound. The parcel is jagged from clearcut. (Ed is pragmatic: "When you need money in the woods, you harvest trees.") The drone of a generator is constant. The cluster of stark, tidy buildings—each painted gray with red trim—is more about service than aesthetics. One structure houses the store and the Raymonds' living quarters; there are two large out-buildings, as well as twin cabins, each with companion privies. The cabins are nothing fancy—gas lamps, particle-board walls, mismatched furnishings, no running water—but they are spotlessly clean, a rigor that applies to pretty much everything in Raymond territory. Aside from the flower arrangements and the life-size plywood moose cutout, you could just as easily be on some forgotten army base.

Inside the store, the lights are bright. The beverage cooler and air conditioner hum, and reruns play on a TV that's built into the wall. The highly varnished pine shelves are stocked with woods groceries: Spam and canned ham, tins of baked beans (vegetarian and regular), loaves of supermarket white and wheat bread, and rows of candy. The cooler is filled with dairy items and soft drinks, as well as a selection of wine and beer, including a couple of microbrews. Gift items—shot glasses, coffee cups, travel mugs, sweatshirts, T-shirts, and a number of moose collec-tables—bear the Northeast Carry name. There's a flat-top griddle for burgers and dogs, and also a pizza carousel. And, of course, there's Ed Raymond, who sports a gray brush cut and can usually be found man-ning the counter or sitting at one of the store's tables regaling a friend or customer (more often than not, one in the same) with a joke or a story. "What's going on next door?" someone asks, referring to the stretch of newly cleared trees on the Raymonds' property. Ed quips: "They're putting in a Wal-Mart." Shirley—who you might have more trouble tracking down—is a compact, wiry woman in her late fifties with thick, short gray hair and a no nonsense air about her. Not that she has a lot of time for foolishness. Ed, who is sixty, has health prob-lems—he has had thirteen cardiac surgeries in the last eleven years, so much of the heavy lifting falls on Shirley's shoulders, and she never lights for long.

When you do get the two together, however, you'll note the rhythm of their banter, with Ed going for the up-front laugh (in regards to his work at the store, he says: "I can't get fired, I don't do anything"); whereas Shirley is more likely to add the wicked aside, often delivered under her breath in her Rhode Island accent. It's this good-natured squabbling, they say, that keeps their relationship healthy—no small concern with this kind of life. It's not that they're completely isolated, though. Depending on the weather, there's satellite TV, cell phone, and an Internet connection. There's the mail—once per week in winter, three times in summer—and the weekly (less often in winter) trips out to provision, mostly to Millinocket, sometimes to Greenville, Bangor, or Augusta. But it certainly helps that they get along so swimmingly.

For Ed, the answer to what brought them to Northeast Carry is automatic. Neither he nor Shirley, who were in their early thirties, had college educations. They could see there was little future for them at the company. Ed, who moved around growing up, had been coming to the family's camp here with his father since he was a boy. Prior to the move, Ed and Shirley had made the ten-hour drive every weekend (save Christmas—that's where Shirley put her foot down) for three years. Why not see what permanent residency had to offer? So, on December 26, 1978, they headed for the woods to test their fate. When they arrived, they had thirteen dollars and change between them.

Raymond's Country Store aside, Northeast Carry is perhaps best known from its mention in *The Maine Woods*, Thoreau's famous chronicle of his passage there. (A carry, so you know, is a portage between two bodies of water—in this case, Moosehead Lake and the West Branch of the Penobscot River.) Because Northeast Carry is fairly easy to traverse—two straight miles with a moderate rise—it served as a crucial link between these two important waterways, first, for Native Americans, then for loggers and sports. The state had established a road there by the early 1800s, which was soon followed by a railway. Early photographs show rails extending out onto a long dock, where cargo that came by rail to Greenville from Bangor and then by steamboat across the lake would be collected into ox-drawn railcars and transported to the river. This was especially important after Chesuncook Dam opened up logging and the need for supplies in the area. A sports camp with hotel and cottages was located at the lake end of the Carry for a time (a couple of the rough structures remain), as were operations for Great Northern Paper, which owned and leased the land on which the current 120 camps and cottages are located. It was also the place the Raymonds decided to call home.

The move was not good news to Shirley's family. The point in life, after all, is to move up in the world, is it not? This taking to the woods was viewed as a backwards step. When Ed and Shirley were finally able to get Shirley's mother to visit, she was ready to turn back by Greenville. They pushed on, but when she arrived at Northeast Carry, she announced she had seen enough—including all the reindeer—and she wished to go home. (She has since come around, says Shirley, adding her parents are proud of all she and Ed have accomplished.)

But you could understand Shirley's mother's feelings, especially if you saw pictures from when the Raymonds first arrived: a portrait of perfect desolation. The muddy, rutted road looked like something from a nineteenth-century mining town. Construction on the buildings had barely begun. (The Raymonds built them all themselves and without one loan. "We don't keep any of the money we earn for ourselves," says Shirley. "We save it toward any upgrading or improvements we would like to make. It takes us a while to reach our goal, but we do get there.") And crowding every photo—nothing but endless scrub and pine. It's obvious whoever was going to make a go at a life here had to possess a great deal of brawn, pluck, and, most important, imagination.

As it turned out, fate played a greater hand in deciding the Raymonds' future than they could've imagined. At first, Ed and Shirley struggled along, doing what they could to get by, mainly selling and delivering propane fuel around the lake. As they became known in the area, people would stop by to see if they had an extra pound of butter or quart of milk they would sell. Soon, it was other forgotten groceries or hardware. The Raymonds, in turn, started buying extra, purchasing, at first, only things they themselves would eat if they didn't sell. An approaching expiration date meant dinner. Using the store as a pantry is a habit that's stayed with them. Ed gets up and grabs a handful of bite-size peppermint patties and distributes them around the table. When he's polished off his stack and reaches for one of Shirley's, his hand is met with a swift smack. "She likes to work, and I like to eat," says Ed. Shirley just rolls her eyes.

The real turning point was when one of their neighbors, who was out snowmobiling with fifteen buddies, stopped by looking for something to eat. You have to understand that, at the time, Ed and Shirley were just barely getting by. (According to Ed, they eked out a whopping $2,500 in earnings their first year.) Their larder wasn't exactly stocked to the rafters, but Shirley rummaged around and put out what they had available: some tuna, cold cuts, and bread. Ed says the only beverage they had to offer was an already-opened bottle of soda and, because there were only four cups, the men had to take turns drinking. But it didn't faze any of them, and their neighbor promised if the Raymonds had food, they'd be back. And he wasn't fooling. They did return. In droves.

And that's because, as anyone in the North Woods can tell you, winter, not summer, is the big season now. When they first arrived, Ed says only eight or ten camps were used in winter. Now he guesses it's ninety-five percent. Shirley says she literally stays up through the weekend to make sure everything—grooming trails ("You don't groom, they won't come"), taking care of the store and the cabins, baking and cooking by night—gets done. She doesn't seem to mind, although she does say by the end of Sunday she starts getting a little punchy.

Of course, there's another vital necessity for sledders, and that's gas. The first gas the Raymonds sold was siphoned out of their own car. Next came a fifty-five-gallon drum that had to be pumped by hand—

fifty strokes per five gallons. From there, they graduated to a 500-gallon tank, and then to their current 12,000-gallon tank, which is housed in a hanger-sized outbuilding with a regulation gas pump and official "Certified Pump Attendant" by the name of Stinky, (a.k.a. Mike Dolan), who earned his name from the skunk cap he wears rather than from any hygiene issue. Mike also does most of the grooming, according to Shirley, and his wife, Carol, helps out with the store. And the help is needed. It's not unusual for two thousand sleds to come through their yard on any given weekend day. Yes, that's two thousand sleds per day. Loneliness is clearly not a problem for the Raymonds.

Transient summer traffic, on the other hand, has dropped off to almost nothing, which further bespeaks the changing character of the North Woods. The Raymonds say they don't even bother renting their cabins in the summer anymore. One reason is the steep gate fees charged by Great North Woods, Inc., a group representing the large, private landowners who control most of the Golden Road and access in the area. Camp owners now have to purchase seasonal or annual registrations. Their guests and other visitors must pay per-person, per-day, access fees ($5 for residents; $8 for non), as well as per-person camping fees, which can quickly add up for a family weekend in the woods.

Another change took place in 2001, when the selling of the camp leases started. While just under ten percent of the camps changed hands and were sold as single-family residences that can't be rented, it marked yet another step away from the patrician days of Great Northern Paper, who used to own the land and maintain the roads and haul trash for the lessees. (Camp owners are now responsible for their own trash and are given no guarantees about the roads.)

It is yet to be seen how this new ownership situation will impact the area, but one thing is sure to remain unchanged: Everyone associated with Northeast Carry depends on the Raymonds. In fact, the sheriff's department calls their store a "contact point," meaning Ed and Shirley can always be relied upon to know who's around and what's going on. This title does not always entail glamorous duties, however.

Death is a big part of their beat. Not long after they arrived, Shirley was enlisted in helping Ed and the game warden get a deceased man in a body bag. When the ordeal was over (the details are not pleasant) and they were back home, Shirley says she looked at Ed and asked (no doubt, in her deadpan), "So, how often does this happen?" But the Raymonds take it all in stride. "Whenever someone dies around Northeast Carry," says Ed, almost cheerfully, "they end up at our store."

Being a contact point also means being the bearer of both good and bad tidings, mostly the latter. It's gotten to the point that Shirley, on her rare days off or moments of leisure, won't go visiting on her own. Residents of Northeast Carry have come to dread seeing her walk into their dooryards.

But Shirley has played an even more crucial role in the woods. While she has no formal medical training, for years she treated any number of ailments and injuries, something she shrugs off with a: "It's a four-hour return rescue to Greenville. What are you going to do?" (Clearing for a helipad in back of their house, however, began in 2003.) If someone needed help, she was often the only option. The Raymonds even purchased an emergency-rescue sled. But because of liability issues, Shirley's doctoring days are over. They've been told all they can do is throw a blanket over the injured party, monitor the injuries, relay what they suspect to the EMTs, and wait for help to arrive. "With one wrong move, we could be wiped out," says Ed. If the person is lucky, he or she will have someone with them who will load them on the rescue sled and take them to the barn, which the Raymonds keep heated for such purposes. They've asked everyone from state officials to insurance reps to look into this, but the verdict, for now, remains the same: Hands off.

When asked if there could be any preparation or training for a life like theirs, Shirley responds: "Preparation? Training? A friend told us to take the first twenty-five dollars we earned and to have our heads checked. Another told us to buy a mirror so we could watch ourselves starve to death. Trial and error is the way we learned. We know we'll never get rich, but we have been happy trying to do things our way."

So, is there anything lacking in their woods life? Ed answers with a resounding "No." He says he never wants to leave Northeast Carry. Shirley, however, takes a minute and thinks. Yes, there is one thing, she says. What could it be? Paved roads? A next-door neighbor? Movie theaters? No. The one thing Shirley Raymond says she misses is ballroom dancing. She almost seems surprised with this admission. But then she smiles, somewhat girlishly, and adds that occasionally she'll turn on the TV when she's alone and dance herself around the room.

And you can bet if you asked her to picture this scenario when she was a girl, you know what her answer would've been . . .

[2004]

Moving Day

Up until this moment, I haven't allowed myself to feel anything. Right now this isn't about me. This is about my mom, who, after fifty years, has decided to leave her 1850s farmhouse in Bath and move into a condominium. Most of her friends have already downsized into smaller, more manageable homes or, in some cases, retirement communities. She is one of the last holdouts. "You'll know when it's time," her friends have said to her as they made their moves. "You'll know when it's time to go." She'd occasionally talk about the idea, but it always began with "I should" (as in, "I should sell this house"), which are, of course, the two words we always use when we have absolutely no intention of doing the thing we're about to say we should.

But then the winter happened. Up until then, my mom had prevailed in the challenge of tending to an old house alone, which she had been doing since my dad died from a sudden and unexpected heart attack in 1985 at the age of sixty-four. My mother is from good Yankee stock, a Gorham girl who knows how to get a job done. She climbs ladders, changes storm windows, shovels, rakes, paints, prunes, and puts up with a grown daughter who still brings her laundry home and has all her stuffed animals, Little Kiddles, Barbies, Tonka trucks, army men, field hockey trophies, yearbooks, old college papers, and prom dresses carelessly stored in the attic. But over the course of that unrelenting and merciless winter, the waiting for the plow and the worrying about ice on the roof, the staying alert for frozen pipes and inspecting for leaks, the lugging of firewood and the sanding of steps just became too much. It was time.

My two older brothers and I readily backed her decision, even though prior to this I was always the one who encouraged her to stay. This was, after all, home. Her neighbors—Bill and Kathy, Bob and Laura Lee—are like family. (If mom's kitchen curtain is not open by seven in the morning, Kathy calls to see what's going on.) There are her beautiful gardens, which have taken years to coax and wrestle out of the miserable Maine clay to consider, and the scent of mock orange and lilac that filters through the kitchen window and fills the house each spring. There's the white-clapboard barn that stands stark against the green-black pines that frame it and the broken weathervane—an outstretched horse racing on the wind—that used to creak every time the weather turned. During the ice storm of 1998, my mother and I watched in silence as an ice-coated pine bough cracked, snapped the weathervane from the cupola, and it bounced in the driveway where I usually park my car. I went out and sifted through the mess until I found the horse, which had held fast atop the vane throughout a century-and-a-half of Maine weather. It was streaked with verdigris, but still intact. I brought it to my mother, and we agreed it could be repaired in the spring, although it remains propped in a corner of her den to this day.

But I haven't yet let myself think about these things. The events surrounding the move happened too quickly. The winter ended, she made her decision, found a new place to live, and put her house on the market. It sold almost instantly to the eldest son of an established Bath family and, somehow, that made it easier. Much better than having the house go to strangers, she said.

After all, this is our family home, the place I was brought to from Bath Memorial Hospital, just a mile up the street. By the time I arrived on the scene, my family was firmly ensconced in the neighborhood, every inch of which I came to know by tagging after my brothers. And there was much to explore: the woods behind our house, where they shot tin cans with BB guns and which led to the back path to Newell School. Across the street, down in back of the Daly's house, was the rubble of North Grammar, which was razed and replaced by Newell just before I started kindergarten. I don't know if they knocked it down with all the contents still inside, but I recall seeing books amid the bricks and pieces of blackboard and plaster, and desks, too, those old-timey, one-piece deals, with the lift-up desktop and hole for the ink bottle – free for the taking. There was still one of those desks, which someone, maybe me, painted white, in my mother's attic.

To our south lived Mrs. Tubbs—at least a hundred years old and rarely seen—in the giant ship-captain's house next door. Woe be to those whose badminton birdie or whiffle ball went over into her yard and had to be retrieved by gingerly scrambling over her fence's sagging, rusted metal framework and splintery railing without getting caught. I don't ever recall being spoken to by Mrs. Tubbs, but I do remember snagging and tearing my shorts on that fence more than once in my attempts to flee as quickly as possible.

To our north lived Eric. Where Mrs. Tubbs was all mystery and shadow, Eric was a wide-open window. He was also at least a hundred, and I was most fascinated by his paucity of teeth and predilection for cats—not to mention the tufts of hair that sprouted from his ears. Very exotic looking to this young child. Eric always had a pipe swung to one side of his mouth, and his wheezy laugh—the sound of air whistling through lightly clenched teeth—was oft-imitated around our house. I knew I could usually find Eric in his yard, which required something of a bushwhack to get to. (This was before my mother got her hands on the greenery on this side of the house.) There he'd be leaning on a rake or shovel, not making much progress on the tangle of weeds and vines his cats darted through, not that he seemed to care much. In fact, I believe he welcomed any distraction, especially if it involved joining my parents for a beer on their patio on a summer Saturday afternoon. I thought this was such an excellent idea that I began issuing the invitation randomly and without consulting my parents, until they had to make clear to me I needed to stop bothering Eric, even though he almost never turned down the offer.

These are but a few of the things I haven't stopped to think about. Although, as I sit here, idling at the intersection at the bottom of our hill and see for the first time the for-sale sign on the front lawn, with a bar across it reading "Sale Pending," I do allow myself a long look up at the house that, for a short while longer, holds my family and its history.

Most adults I know do not have this luxury. They do not sleep in their old bedroom when they visit their parents. They do not test themselves to see if they can still walk the entire house in the pitch-black dark. They do not go to retrieve something from the den closet and smell the same smell of sewing basket/vacuum cleaner/handbag they have since childhood. They do not glimpse from the corner of their eye the memory image of their father just inside the barn door. Or cradle the familiar smooth cool of a porcelain doorknob. Or smile at the small crack in the hall window, where a hurled building block hit just after missing their brother's head. Or hear the remembered creak of a weathervane as it wheeled in the night. Most of the adults I know have long ago had this moment of reckoning, and I should be ready for mine.

Besides, there's 175 square feet of bubble wrap and a roll of packing tape in the back of my car and work to be done. I release the brake and head for home.

[2003]

About the Author

In the event there could possibly be anything else you wanted to know about Elizabeth Peavey, she is a contributing editor to *Down East* magazine. Her essays and articles have also appeared in *Yankee's Travel Guide to New England*, *Maine Boats & Harbors*, and *Odyssey Travel*, among others. She authored the chapter on Maine for Fodor's *Road Guide U.S.A.* and has contributed essays to the Maine Public Radio program "Maine Things Considered." Her humor column, "Outta My Way," ran in the Portland alternative paper *Casco Bay Weekly* for six years. She has taught creative writing at the University of Maine at Farmington and teaches public speaking at the University of Southern Maine. In 1995, she was a member of the Maine Slam Poetry Team that came in fourth in the nation. She lives with her husband in Portland, Maine. And, she likes beer.